# Classroom Reading Games Activities Kit

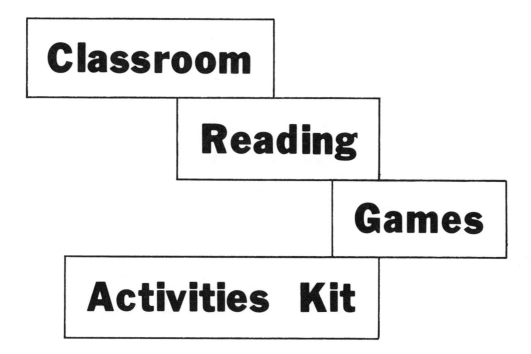

# Classroom Reading Games Activities Kit

## JERRY J. MALLETT

The Center for Applied Research in Education, Inc.
521 Fifth Avenue, New York, N.Y. 10017

**Library of Congress Cataloging in Publication Data**

Mallett, Jerry J
   Classroom reading games activities kit.

   1.  Reading (Elementary)  2.  Reading games.
I.  Title.
LB1573.M32        372.4'14        74-28176
ISBN 0-87628-206-0

Printed in the United States of America

*I wish to dedicate this book to David, Christopher, and Michael. Through dedicated and creative teachers, they already know that learning can be exciting and fun.*

# About the Author

Jerry J. Mallett, Ed.D., has been actively involved in elementary education for more than ten years as a classroom teacher, reading specialist, and school principal. The author of nine articles on reading and language arts in professional journals, Dr. Mallett is also a contributing editor to the *Ohio Reading Teacher* and a field representative of the Ohio International Reading Association.

Awarded his doctorate by the University of Toledo in 1972, Dr. Mallett is presently Associate Professor of Elementary Education at Findlay College, Findlay, Ohio.

# About the Author

Jerry J. Mallett, Ed.D., has been actively involved in elementary education for more than ten years as a classroom teacher, reading specialist, and school principal. The author of nine articles on reading and language arts in professional journals, Dr. Mallett is also a contributing editor to the *Ohio Reading Teacher* and a field representative of the Ohio International Reading Association.

Awarded his doctorate by the University of Toledo in 1972, Dr. Mallett is presently Associate Professor of Elementary Education at Findlay College, Findlay, Ohio.

# About This Aid

The purpose of the *Classroom Reading Games Activities Kit* is to help you meet the needs of *all* of your students in the teaching of specific reading skills. While it is meant to help the teacher individualize his or her reading program, the author would not like to see any teacher overemphasize the skills at the expense of a child-centered classroom. No technique or game can ever take the place of a warm, understanding, and compassionate teacher.

To help you in selecting appropriate activities for the individual child or group, this aid is organized according to the following developmental reading skills:

1. Readiness
2. Sight Word Knowledge
3. Phonetic Analysis
4. Structural Analysis
5. Comprehension
6. Critical Reading Skills

In addition, all of the games in the *Classroom Reading Games Activities Kit* include broad grade-level standards, and the progression of skills activities in each section is sequenced from easiest to more difficult. Within a class of thirty youngsters, children will be found at varying degrees along the developmental skills continuum. Therefore, it is not as important to know the grade level of each skill as it is to match the right skill with the particular student.

*Jerry J. Mallett*

# Contents

# Contents

**Structural Analysis,** *(cont.)*

**5    Comprehension** ...................................163

# Contents

# Using These Reading Games Most Effectively

**Organizing Game Materials**

For effective use of the following reading games, each individual game should be kept in its own container. This container might be either a large manila envelope or a box. Boxes are the more durable and lend themselves to better classroom organization. Most department stores will provide boxes but ditto-master boxes are better since they are constructed of heavier cardboard. It is wise to cover the boxes with Contac paper. By using the following method, the Contac paper will protect your boxes, helping them to last through many years of use.

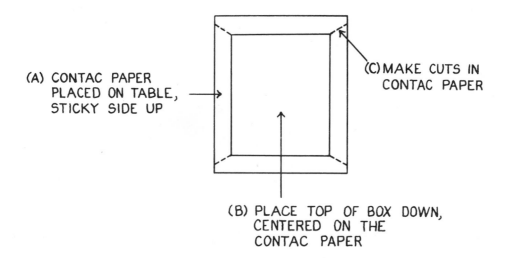

(A) CONTAC PAPER PLACED ON TABLE, STICKY SIDE UP

(C) MAKE CUTS IN CONTAC PAPER

(B) PLACE TOP OF BOX DOWN, CENTERED ON THE CONTAC PAPER

(D) AFTER MAKING CUTS IN THE CONTAC PAPER, FOLD EACH END OVER AND AROUND THE CORNERS

(E) YOU WILL HAVE TO AGAIN CUT THE CONTAC PAPER AT EACH CORNER IN ORDER TO FOLD IT INTO THE BOX

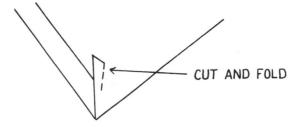

CONTAC          BOX

CUT AND FOLD

# Using These Reading Games

For easy identification of the games, label the envelopes and/or boxes with (a) a reading area color code, and (b) the title of the specific reading game. It is a good idea to number the games also. The labeling should be located at the top of the envelopes and at the end of the boxes.

To label the materials, use a black, fine-tip marking pen to letter the title of the specific reading game and its corresponding number on an unlined index card. Then, using either marking pens or colored tape, place the appropriate color code on the index card as shown below.

| Color Code | Number of Game | Title of Reading Game |
|---|---|---|
| | | |

In order to do this, simply decide upon one color to represent each reading area. You will need six colors, since all of the game activities in this aid are divided into six major reading areas: Readiness, Sight Word Knowledge, Phonetic Analysis, Structural Analysis, Comprehension, and Critical Reading Skills. Color coding each game not only helps both the teacher and the students to quickly find the appropriate game, but also assures its return to the proper reading area.

Finally, cut the index card to size and glue it on the end of the appropriate box. If you are using envelopes, simply put the information directly on the envelope.

## Assigning Games to Meet Specific Individual Needs

Students should be given *gradual* freedom to use the reading game activities. At first you might want to set up specific times within which they could be used, such as during reading seatwork time. But once children have developed a maturity and routine in using the games, the time might be expanded throughout the school day.

Begin the procedure with only a few reading games in your room. Spend ample time in explaining the procedure and have a few "dry runs." Be sure to explain each game to the class and continue to thoroughly explain additional game activities as you increase their numbers throughout the year. This will save you much time and many questions in the future.

The author would recommend that students be assigned specific games rather than be given a complete freedom of choice in using them. Those assigned should reinforce certain skills with which a child is experiencing difficulty or is just learning. In this manner a teacher is able to guide each child through his own needs but still maintain a sequential order in the developmental reading skills.

One of the simplest ways to correlate specific reading game aids to the individual student's needs is use of the Flexible Aid Chart. The chart itself may be placed on one of the classroom bulletin boards and consists of (1) a permanent alphabetical listing of your students' names and (2) the three columns to the right of the class list shown in the illustration on the following page.

|  | *Today's Aids* | *If You Have Time* | *Results* |
|---|---|---|---|
| **Brown, John** |  |  |  |
| **Candle, Sue** |  |  |  |
| **Dove, James** |  |  |  |
| **Earl, Frank** |  |  |  |
| **Glick, Ann** |  |  |  |

**FLEXIBLE AID CHART**

In order to save time in the use of this technique, make a minimum of three "title cards" for each game that you have available in the classroom. These must be small enough so that two or three may easily fit within each of the columns on the Flexible Aid Chart. The title cards should contain (1) the name of the reading game activity, (2) its number, and (3) the color code of the appropriate skill area. (The title card will last much longer if you print them on lightweight posterboard and then laminate the cards.)

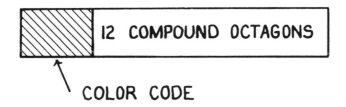

12 COMPOUND OCTAGONS

COLOR CODE

Also make a store of "result cards." These are cards the student uses to inform you of his day's progress. Result cards are of two types: (1) Finished, and (2) In Progress. The student simply places the "title card" along with the appropriate "result card" in the *Results* column on the Flexible Aid Chart. It is assumed that those title cards left in either of the other two columns (*Today's Aids/If You Have Time*) at the end of the school day were not started by the student.

By using the Flexible Aid Chart technique the teacher is able to make the day's assignments easily and quickly and also to keep informed as to the day's progress of each child. With this information, plus the insight gained during the day's activities, the teacher is in a fairly good position to organize the next day's assignments and activities.

# 1 · Readiness

As teachers we all too often associate "readiness" with those activities that take place during the kindergarten experience. After the year in kindergarten the children are then placed in a formal reading program with the "readiness stage" seemingly finished. The author does not accept this idea of readiness. Instead he believes that the concept of readiness should be extended upward to all grades. Even though readiness has been achieved during the kindergarten experience, it does not necessarily follow that readiness is retained at a higher level of experience. There sometimes is needed concern with readiness at the first, second, and third-grade levels.

Therefore, it is recommended that teachers using this aid view this section on readiness not as one to be used only at the kindergarten and first-grade levels but, rather, as an aid to be used with all students who need the activities, regardless of grade level.

# Look-alikes

## Materials Needed:

posterboard—15 pieces 3″ × 4″
felt-tipped pen
scissors

## Making the Game:

Copy the following on the pieces of tagboard.

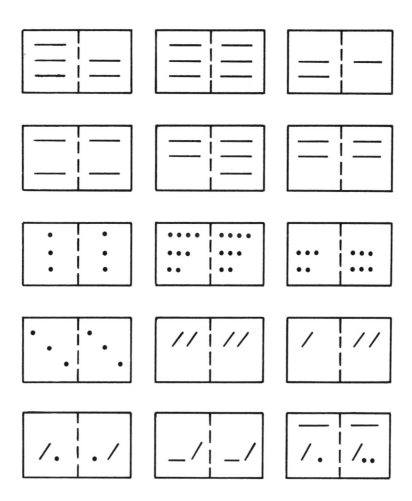

Place smiling faces on the backs of those cards that have two marks that are the same, and frowning faces on the backs of the cards that have different marks.

# *Readiness*

## Student Game Directions:

1. There are two sides on each card. Each side has marks on it. Some cards have two sides that are the same.

2. Find the cards that have the same marks on either side and place them in one pile.

3. Place the other cards in another pile.

4. Check your work. Turn the cards over. On the back you will see either a smiling face or a frowning face. Those cards that have two marks that are the same have smiling faces on their back side. Those cards that have marks that are different have frowning faces on their back side.

# Alphabet Oak Tree

## Materials Needed:

posterboard— 1 piece 13″ × 8″
                26 pieces 1¼″ × 1″
felt-tipped pen
scissors

## Making the Game:

Cut out the following tree design using the 13″ × 8″ piece of tagboard.

Print the upper-case alphabet on the tree.

Cut the small pieces of posterboard into the shape of acorns. (See the pattern below.)

Print the lower-case alphabet on the small pieces of posterboard.

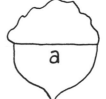

## Student Game Directions:

1. Place the tree on a flat surface.

2. Take the acorns and match the letter on each acorn with its capital letter on the tree.

3. Have someone check your work.

# Matching Beginning Sounds

## Materials Needed:

posterboard—26 pieces 3″ × 3″
felt-tipped pen
pictures emphasizing the sounds that are being studied
tape or glue

## Making the Game:

Print the letters of the alphabet on the pieces of posterboard.

Dry mount or glue the pictures on pieces of posterboard.

## Student Game Directions:

1. Make two piles, one with letter cards and one with picture cards. You will need a flat surface to work on.

2. Spread out the alphabet letters on your desk in a straight line.

3. Look at one picture at a time. Say the name of the picture. What letter does the word begin with?

4. Place the picture under the alphabet letter that is the beginning letter of that word.

5. When you are finished, turn the picture cards over. If the letter on the back matches the alphabet letter, you have done it right.

# Grapheme Match

## Materials Needed:

posterboard—8 pieces 6″ × 9″
scissors

## Making the Game:

Fold and cut the posterboard pieces as shown.

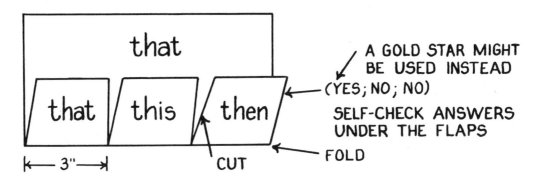

Under the flap that has the correct word on the front, place the word YES. Under the flaps of the other two words place the word NO. This will be used so that the student may correct himself.

Copy the following words on the remaining seven game boards.

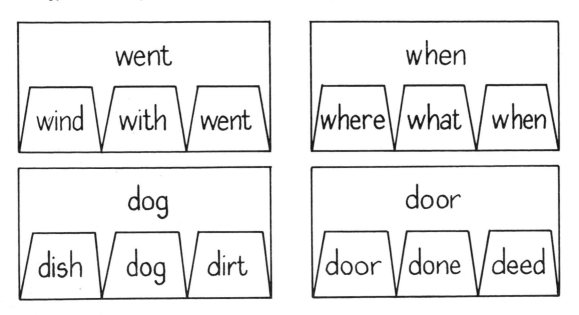

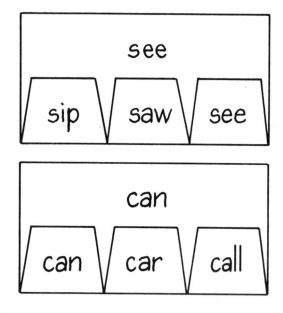
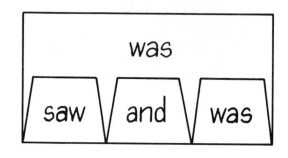

## Student Game Directions:

1. Look at the cards carefully.

2. Now look at the top word. See if you can find another word on that card that matches the top word.

3. When you think you have found it, lift up the flap that the word is on. If there is a YES (or a gold star) under it you are correct. If not, try again.

# What Is Missing?

## Materials Needed:

posterboard— 8 pieces 4″ × 10″
                26 pieces 2″ × 2″
ruler
felt-tipped pen
scissors

## Making the Game:

Fold the 4″ × 10″ pieces of posterboard to make 2″ × 10″ rectangles. Using a ruler, draw a line every two inches as shown.

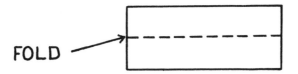

Copy the following letters on the posterboard pieces.

Cut out the squares that would cover the letters if folded over. On the back of the blank letter spaces copy the letter that has been omitted so that if it is folded over it will show the correct letter.

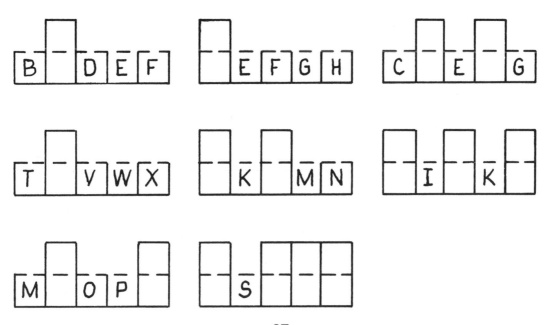

# *Readiness*

## Student Game Directions:

1. Take one strip at a time. Look at the letters. There are one or more letters missing in the order they are in.

2. Find the missing letters from the letter cards and place them in the blank spaces.

3. Now fold the squares over to see if you are right.

# Match the Letters

## Materials:

posterboard— 2 pieces 6″ × 10″
             52 pieces 1″ × 1″
felt-tipped pen

## Making the Game:

Print the upper and lower-case alphabet on the 1″ × 1″ pieces of posterboard.

Print the letters of the alphabet on the 6″ × 10″ pieces of posterboard, the upper case on one and the lower case on the other as in the accompanying illustrations.

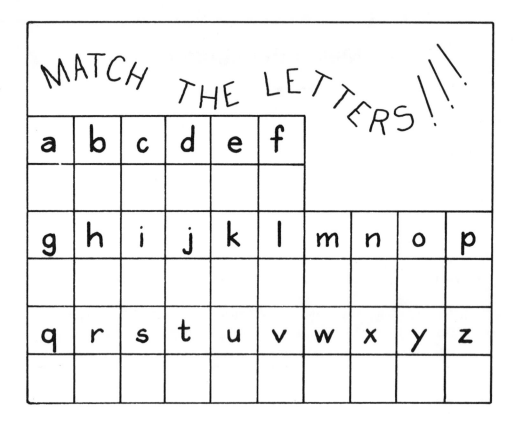

## Student Game Directions:

1. Take out the big cards and place them in front of you.

2. Decide which card you will use. If you use the card with the capital letters then you must place the small cards with the small letters under each capital letter. If you use the card with the small letters then you must place the small cards with the capital letters under each small letter.

3. Have someone check your card when you are finished.

# Family Belongings

## Materials Needed:

posterboard
pictures
scissors
tape or glue

## Making the Game:

Cut out the following pictures from either readiness books, magazines, or catalogs.

> 1. family group
> 2. father
> 3. mother
> 4. boy
> 5. girl
> 6. baby

Cut out pictures of items that any one member of the family or the family as a whole would use.

Dry mount or glue these pictures on the posterboard.

## Student Game Directions:

1. Find the pictures of the members of the family.

2. Place them on your desk or table across the top.

3. Now place all the items under the picture of the family member who would most likely use them.

4. If more than one member of the family would use one particular item, place it under the picture of the family group.

# Winter Fun—Summer Fun

## Materials Needed:

posterboard
pictures
scissors
tape or glue

## Making the Game:

Cut out pictures of items or scenes of activities (snow skiing, etc.) that depict either the summer season or the winter season.

Dry mount or glue these pictures on the posterboard.

## Student Game Directions:

1. Turn the pictures face up on your desk,

2. Now separate the pictures into two groups. The pictures that have something to do with the winter season go in one stack and the pictures that have something to do with the summer season go in another stack.

# Configuration Match

## Materials Needed:

posterboard—10 pieces 12″ × 4″

               10 pieces  3″ × 4″

ruler

felt-tipped pen

scissors

## Making the Game:

Fold the 12″ × 4 ″ pieces of posterboard three inches from the top.

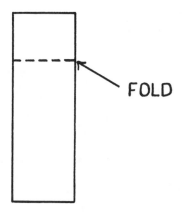

Put the following words on the bottom section of the 12″ × 4″ pieces of posterboard.

then
what
where
that
is
it
did
does
why
yes

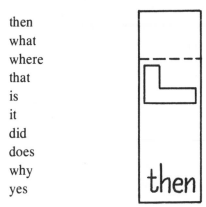

# *Readiness*

Put the following configuration drawings on the second section of the 12″ × 4″ piece of posterboard so that the flap section covers it. Cut the same patterns out of the 3″ × 4″ pieces of posterboard.

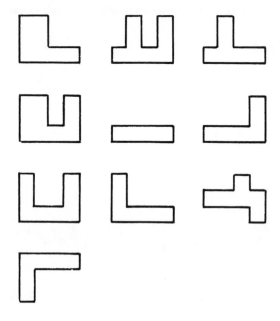

## Student Game Directions:

1. Place all of the small configuration cards on your desk.

2. Take one of the large folded cards and place it on your desk.

3. Look at the word at the bottom of this large card. Notice its shape. Now find the small configuration card that has the same shape.

4. Do the same with all the other cards.

5. You may check your answer by lifting up the folded section of the large card and seeing if the small configuration card fits in the outline.

# Listen and Jump

## Materials Needed:

posterboard—32 pieces 3″ × 3″
oilcloth—1 piece 4″ × 4″
yardstick
felt-tipped pen

## Making the Game:

Put the following lines and letters on the oilcloth.

| G | L | M | D |
|---|---|---|---|
| R | H | F | P |
| Y | S | W | K |
| C | N | T | J |

# Readiness

Put the following drawings on the 3″ × 3″ posterboard pieces.

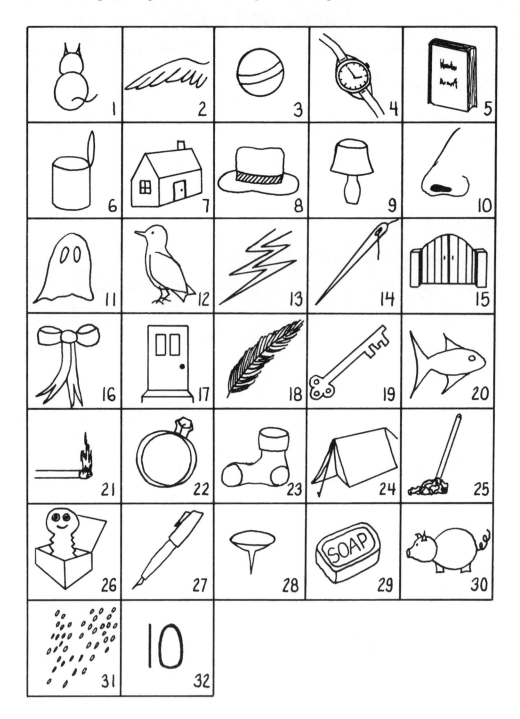

Write the following checklist on the inside of the top of the box or on a piece of posterboard.

ANSWER SHEET

| | | | | | |
|---|---|---|---|---|---|
| 1 C | 6 C | 11 G | 16 B | 21 M | 26 J |
| 2 W | 7 H | 12 B | 17 D | 22 R | 27 P |
| 3 B | 8 H | 13 L | 18 F | 23 S | 28 T |
| 4 W | 9 L | 14 N | 19 K | 24 T | 29 S |
| 5 B | 10 N | 15 G | 20 F | 25 M | 30 P |
| | | | | | 31 R |
| | | | | | 32 T |

## Student Game Directions:

1. Choose a friend to play this game with you.

2. Place the oilcloth on the floor.

3. Turn the cards over so that you cannot see the pictures.

4. Now choose a card and turn it over. Say the word and jump to the letter that has the same sound as the beginning of the word.

5. Check the answer on the answer check sheet to see if you are correct. If you are correct, you score one point. Now it's your partner's turn.

6. The person who has the most points when all of the cards have been used is the winner.

# Egg Carton Toss

## Materials Needed:

2 buttons
egg carton
posterboard—30 pieces 3″ × 3″
felt-tipped pen

## Making the Game:

Print the following consonants in the egg carton as shown in the following illustration:

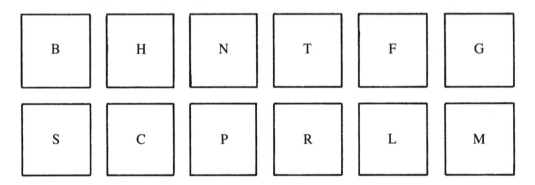

Put the following drawings on the pieces of posterboard.

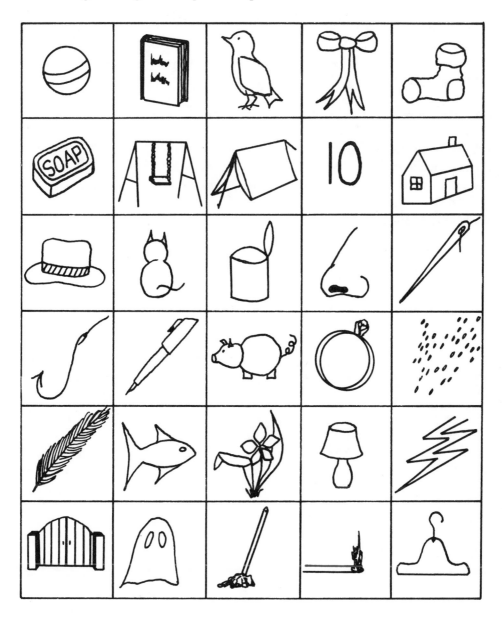

## Student Game Directions:

1. Choose a friend to play this game with you.

2. Decide who will go first. Place the egg carton on the floor about three feet away from yourselves.

3. Place the posterboard pieces on a flat surface with the pictures up.

4. Take turns tossing the button into the egg carton. If you miss, the other person tries. If you get the button in a cup, you must find a posterboard picture that begins with the letter's sound. If you do this, you keep the picture.

5. When you finish, the person with the most cards is the winner.

# 2 · Sight Word Knowledge

If our English language were truly phonetic, that is, each phoneme or sound was represented by one and only one grapheme or symbol, then the teaching of reading and spelling would be simple, indeed. As a matter of fact, spelling need not be taught in those countries where language is phonetic in nature. If a child has good auditory discrimination and can hear the various sounds within a word, he can spell that word correctly. Spelling then becomes the simple task of matching the appropriate letter to the particular sound.

Unfortunately, the English language does not provide us with such a phonetic pattern. For instance, the sound of the long *a* may be spelled several different ways; as in the words *fa*te, *d*ay, th*ey*, *s*ail, r*ei*gn, and gr*ea*t. Or the word "fish" could be phonetically spelled "ghoti." The *gh* would be sounded as in rou*gh*, the *o* would be sounded as in w*o*men, and the *ti* would be sounded as in na*ti*on.

Consequently, a reading technique has de-veloped in our schools that is known as the "look-say" or "whole-word" method. This method recognizes the fact that many of the words in our English language are nonphonetic in structure. Therefore, these words must be memorized through repetition and are commonly referred to as sight words. Words with indefinite meanings such as "of," those with difficult phonetic combinations such as "one," and some proper names are examples of sight words. Certain words such as "grandmother," "elephant," and "Christmas," will be remembered after only a few repetitions, but other words need many repetitions before they are mastered. Words like "here," "there," "who," "what," and "where" are especially difficult.

It is therefore the purpose of this section to offer the teacher a variety of games and activities that will provide the necessary drill for sight word memorization.

# More of the Same

*(Low Primary)*

## Materials Needed:

posterboard—1 piece 4″ × 6″
newspaper or/and magazine articles
scissors
glue

## Making the Game:

Select five words that have been introduced recently in reading. These should be words to be learned by sight and not phonics.

Cut out several of these words from the articles and glue them on the piece of posterboard.

## Student Game Directions:

1. Place the piece of posterboard with the words on your desk.

2. Look through the papers in the box and cut out all of the words that are the same.

3. You may glue them on another piece of paper if you like.

# Picture-Word Slide

*(Low Primary)*

## Materials Needed:

posterboard—1 piece 6″ × 10″
                6 pieces 2″ × 12″ (2 each of 3 different colors)
ruler
scissors
felt-tipped pen

## Making the Game:

Cut 2″ slits in the 6″ × 10″ piece of posterboard as shown.

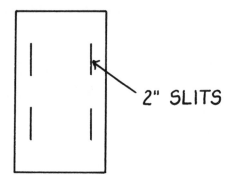

2″ SLITS

Put the following on the 2″ × 12″ pieces of posterboard. Make sure that the pairs of strips are on the same color posterboard.

## Student Game Directions:

1. Take the large piece of posterboard out of the box.

2. Select two long strips of posterboard of the same color. Place the long strips through the slits in the large piece of posterboard so that they slide back and forth. Be sure the strips are of the same color.

3. Select one of the pictures on the picture strip. Now slide the other strip until you find the word that says the name of the picture.

4. Match all of the pictures and words on the strips.

# Picture Triangle Twist
*(Primary)*

## Materials Needed:

posterboard— 5 pieces 4″ × 4″ (red)
15 pieces 4″ × 4″ (yellow)
ruler
scissors
felt-tipped pen

## Making the Game:

Cut triangles from the posterboard pieces. Use the following pattern.

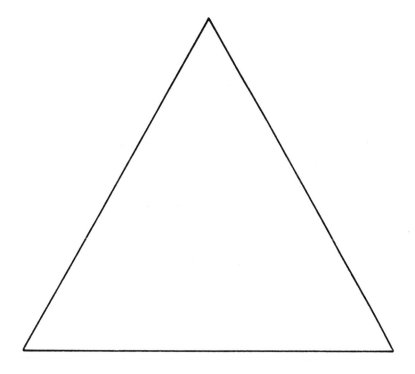

# Sight Word Knowledge

Print the following words on the red triangles as shown. Print one definition on each of the yellow triangles as shown.

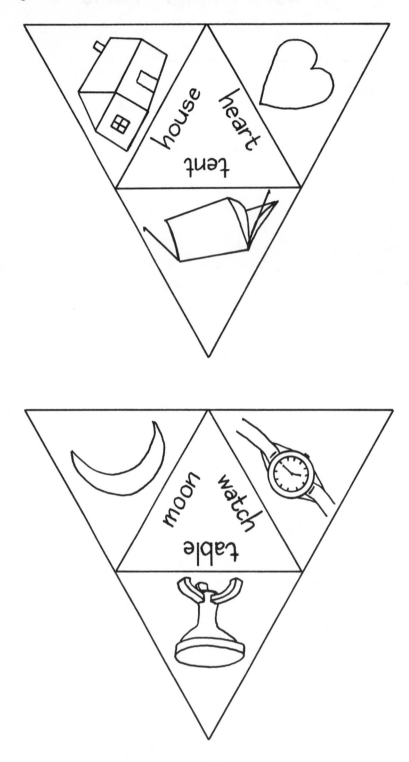

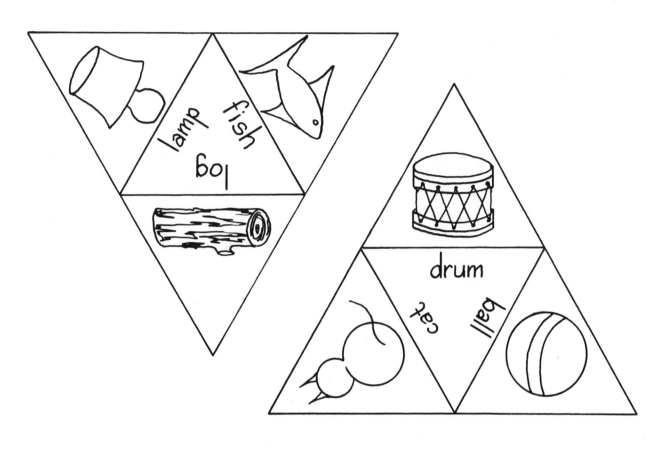

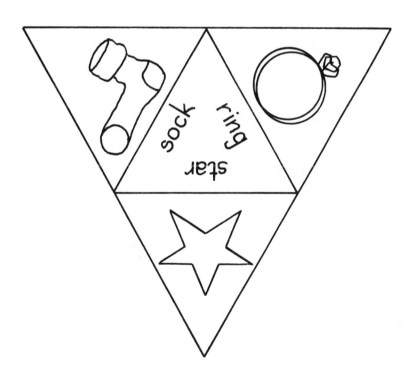

# Sight Word Knowledge

## Student Game Directions:

1. Take a red triangle out of the box and place it face up on your desk.

2. Now place the yellow triangles face up on your desk. Choose one of the words on your red triangle. Find a picture on a yellow triangle that shows what the word means.

3. Place that yellow picture triangle next to the red word triangle as shown below:

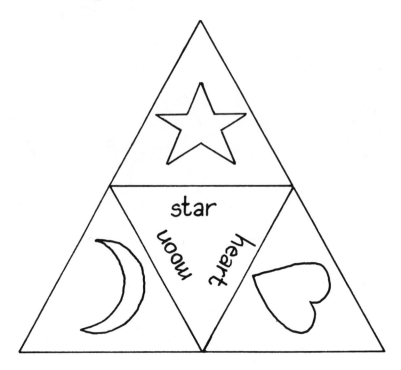

4. Continue this until all of the yellow pictures triangles have been matched with the red word triangles.

5. Have someone check your work.

# Opposites
## *(Primary)*

## Materials Needed:

posterboard—16 pieces 2″ × 4″ (red)
        16 pieces 2″ × 4″ (green)
felt-tipped pen

## Making the Game:

Put the following words on the red posterboard pieces.

> hot, lose, summer, easy, rough, go, slow, low, quiet, light, south, day, weak, difficult, short, sister

Put the following words on the green posterboard pieces.

> north, high, strong, heavy, fast, easy, noisy, cold, hard, win, winter, smooth, come, tall, night, brother

## Student Game Directions:

1. Separate the green cards from the red cards.

2. Take one pile and look at the first word.

3. Take the other pile and find a word that means the opposite of the first word.

4. Have someone play with you. Test each other.

5. If you are playing by yourself, have someone check your work.

# Classifying Words

*(Primary)*

## Materials Needed:

posterboard— 3 pieces 8″ × 10″
24 pieces 2″ × 5″
scissors
felt-tipped pen

## Making the Game:

Cut the 8″ × 10″ pieces of posterboard in the following shape and label each ''store'' as shown.

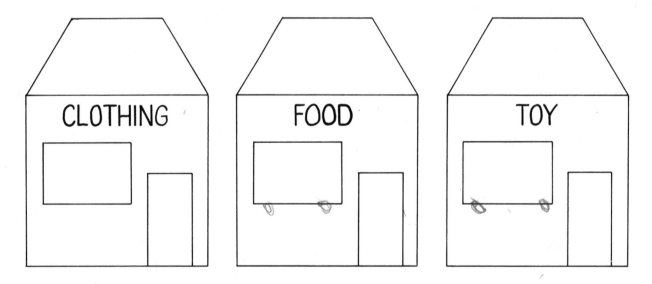

Put the following words on the 2″ × 5″ pieces of posterboard.

| | | | | |
|---|---|---|---|---|
| pants | donuts | train | shoes | beans |
| wagon | hat | steak | marbles | dress |
| bread | crayons | socks | chicken | ball |
| tie | milk | kite | shirt | potatoes |
| bat | belt | bicycle | hot dog | |

## Student Game Directions:

1. Place the store cards out on your desk or another flat surface.

2. Take the item cards and place them under the store in which you would find them sold.

3. Have someone check your work.

# Spinner Winner

*(Primary)*

## Materials Needed:

posterboard—1 piece 10″ × 16″
one spinner
two or more markers (pieces to move on the gameboard)
ruler
felt-tipped pen

## Making the Game:

Lay out a gameboard as shown in the illustration on page 55.

## Student Game Directions:

1. Two people play this game at a time.

2. Place the markers on START. Each person spins the spinner to see who goes first (the higher number).

3. Spin the spinner and move the number of spaces it says. Say the words on the space or follow the directions. If you say the words wrong, you do not move.

4. The first person to reach square 35 is the winner.

| | 2<br><br>did<br>take | 3<br><br>move<br>ahead<br>five<br>spaces | 4<br><br>also<br>boy<br>her | 5<br><br>it<br>them<br>away |
|---|---|---|---|---|
| START | | | | |
| 6<br><br>of<br>old | 7<br><br>then<br>work<br>your<br>high | 8<br><br>go<br>back<br>two<br>spaces | 9<br><br>go<br>back<br>to<br>START | 10<br><br>get<br>for<br>had |
| 11<br><br>am<br>was<br>out | 12<br><br>move<br>back<br>three<br>spaces | 13<br><br>my<br>not<br>the | 14<br><br>she<br>come | 15<br><br>five<br>far |
| 16<br><br>got<br>let | 17<br><br>of<br>move<br>tell | 18<br><br>too<br>in | 19<br><br>their<br>if | 20<br><br>go<br>good |
| 21<br><br>put<br>some | 22<br><br>go<br>back<br>ten<br>spaces | 23<br><br>three<br>two | 24<br><br>very<br>that | 25<br><br>each<br>best |
| 26<br><br>big<br>left | 27<br><br>go<br>back<br>two<br>spaces | 28<br><br>should<br>have<br>can | 29<br><br>this<br>these | 30<br><br>their<br>the<br>this<br>there |
| 31<br><br>it<br>if<br>is<br>get | 32<br><br>at<br>cat<br>bat<br>hat | 33<br><br>by<br>high<br>lie<br>sight | 34<br><br>witch<br>which<br>took<br>take | 35<br><br>WINNER |

# Sound Words

## *(Primary)*

## Materials Needed:

posterboard—10 pieces 5″ × 5″
             10 pieces 2″ by length of word
felt-tipped pen
scissors

## Making the Game:

Copy the following sound words on the 2″ pieces of posterboard.

   oink, tick tock, ding dong, click, honk, ring, purr, drip, bang, moo

Using the following patterns, cut out the objects from the 5″ posterboard pieces. Print the names on the objects as shown.

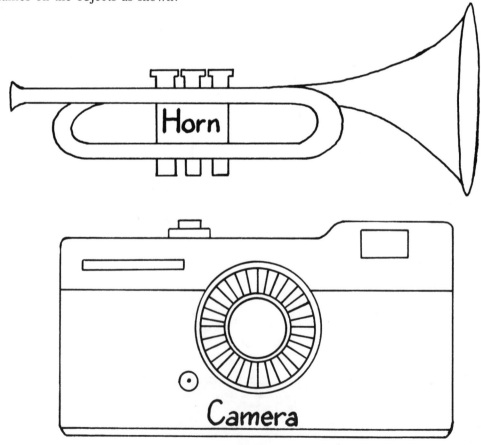

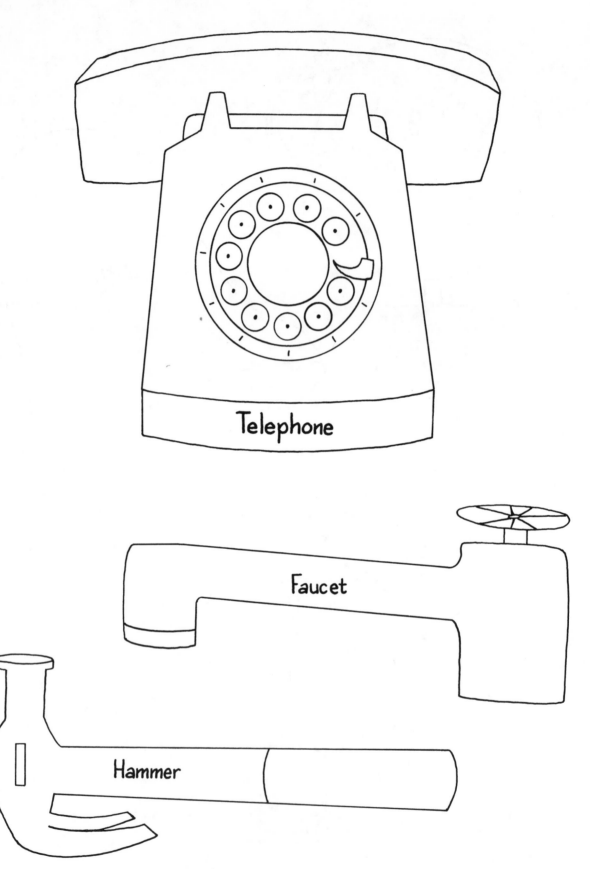

Telephone

Faucet

Hammer

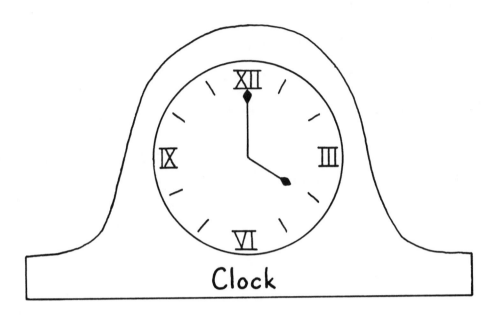

Clock

Cow

*Sight Word Knowledge*

## Student Game Directions:

1. Place the objects face up on your desk.

2. Turn all the word cards face up on your desk.

3. Try to match the sound word with the object that you think would most likely make that sound.

4. When you are finished, turn the objects and word cards over. If you were correct, the numbers on the backs will match.

# Find the Picture

*(Primary)*

## Materials Needed:

posterboard— 1 piece 7½" × 16"
                15 pieces 1¼" × 1¼"
pictures
glue or tape
ruler
felt-tipped pen

## Making the Game:

Glue or dry mount the pictures on the small pieces of posterboard.

Make the following gameboard.

FOLD

| 1. cat 2. dog 3. fish | 1 | 2 | 3 |
|---|---|---|---|
| 4. doll 5. ball 6. car | 4 | 5 | 6 |
| 7. airplane 8. bicycle 9. wagon | 7 | 8 | 9 |
| 10. scissors 11. rake 12. mop | 10 | 11 | 12 |
| 13. shoes 14. boy 15. girl | 13 | 14 | 15 |

SELF-CHECK

Do not lift until you are finished

## Student Game Directions:

1. Take out the gameboard. Be sure the self-check is folded over.

2. On the side is a list of words.

3. You must match the picture card with the word it represents. Place the correct picture in the square having the same number as the word.

4. Fold back the self-check and see if you are correct.

# Number-Picture Match

*(Primary)*

## Materials Needed:

posterboard— 1 piece 7″ × 14″
               5 pieces 1″ × 2″
picture—about 6″ × 6″
glue
felt-tipped pen

## Making the Game:

Select a picture showing various items, and glue the picture to the 7″ × 14″ gameboard as shown.

Set up the rest of the gameboard similar to the board in the illustration with a list of words naming items in the picture and another list of numbers with arrows pointing to the same items in the picture.

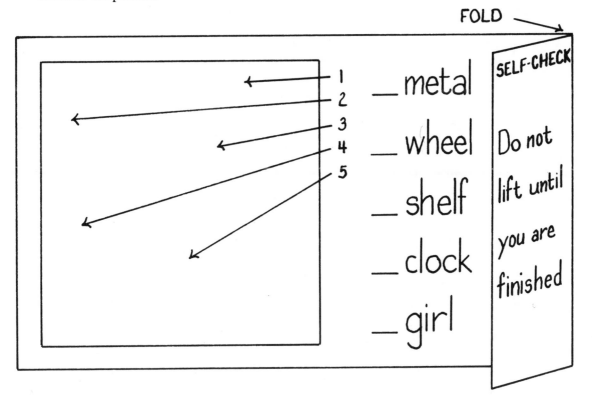

Number the 1″ × 2″ posterboard pieces one through five.

# Sight Word Knowledge

## Student Game Directions:

1. Take the gameboard out of the box. Be sure that the self-check is folded over.

2. Look at the picture. You see arrows pointing to things in the picture. Each arrow has a number next to it.

3. Now look at the list of words. Each word names one of the things in the picture.

4. Choose an arrow pointing to one of the things and then find the word in the list that names it.

5. Take the correct number card and place it next to the word that it represents in the picture.

6. Continue through all the words.

7. Lift the self-check and correct yourself.

# Alphabetizing Categories
## *(High Primary)*

## Materials Needed:

posterboard— 3 pieces 2″ × 6″
              30 pieces 2″ × 4″
felt-tipped pen

## Making the Game:

Put the following categories on the 2″ × 6″ pieces:

FOODS     COUNTRIES     ANIMALS

Put the following words on the 2″ × 4″ pieces of posterboard.

milk, ham, eggs, carrot, peas, beans, cabbage, lettuce, tomato, spinach, pig, cat, cow, horse, goat, wolf, snake, beetle, rat, fox, Scotland, Austria, Australia, Spain, England, Greece, Egypt, Italy, China, Japan

## Student Game Directions:

1. Pick out the larger cards and spread them out in alphabetical order on a flat surface. These are your category cards.

2. Now take the small cards and place them under the correct categories.

3. Then take each category and alphabetize the words in it.

4. Have someone check your work.

# Classifying Nouns

*(Upper Primary)*

## Materials Needed:

posterboard—30 pieces 2″ × 5″ (15 yellow and 15 green)
felt-tipped pen

## Making the Game:

On the yellow cards put the words PERSON, PLACE, and THING five times each.

Put the following words on the green cards.

> Florida, Ohio, New York, Michigan, Utah, John, Sally, Bill, Dave, Mike, cap, coat, nickel, umbrella, ticket

## Student Game Directions:

1. Take out the cards that say PERSON, PLACE, and THING (yellow cards).

2. Now take out the green cards. Take one of the green cards and read the word on it. Is it a person, place, or thing? When you have decided, place an appropriate yellow card next to it.

3. Continue to do the rest.

4. Have someone check your work before you put it away.

# Holiday Words

*(High Primary–Low Intermediate)*

## Materials Needed:

posterboard— 3 pieces 8″ × 10″
　　　　　　 24 pieces 2″ × 5″
scissors
felt-tipped pen

## Making the Game:

Cut the following forms from the 8″ × 10″ pieces of posterboard.

Put the following words on the 2″ × 5″ pieces of posterboard.

　　ghost, broom, bats, jack-o-lanterns, skeleton, black cat, trick-or-treat, goblin,
　　turkey, pilgrim, feast, cranberry, harvest, horn of plenty, presents, ornaments,
　　angel, star, Santa Claus, tinsel, reindeer, mistletoe

*Sight Word Knowledge*

## Student Game Directions:

1. Think of all the different words that you might associate with Halloween, Thanksgiving, and Christmas.

2. There are many words in the box and all of them have something to do with Halloween, Thanksgiving, and Christmas.

3. Look at the words and place them under the correct heading.

4. Have someone check your work.

# Words Have Feelings

*(High Primary–Low Intermediate)*

## Materials Needed:

posterboard— 4 pieces 4″ × 4″
                      32 pieces 2″ × 6″
scissors
felt-tipped pen

## Making the Game:

Using the 4″ × 4″ pieces of posterboard, cut out circles with 4″ diameters.

Put the following faces on the circles.

Put the following words on the 2″ × 6″ pieces of posterboard.

| | | | | |
|---|---|---|---|---|
| happy | glad | cheerful | delighted | joyful |
| pleased | worried | scared | satisfied | frightened |
| contented | concerned | troubled | anxious | nervous |
| frantic | disturbed | sad | unhappy | downcast |
| gloomy | blue | sorrowful | miserable | melancholy |
| proud | haughty | vain | smug | egotistical |
| conceited | | | | |

# Sight Word Knowledge

## Student Game Directions:

1. Take out the faces and place them on your desk.

2. Take one word card. Read the word. What feeling does the word have? Would it go with a happy face? If so, place it under the happy face. Continue with the rest of the word cards.

3. Have someone check your work.

# Fishing for Words

*(Primary–Low Intermediate)*

## Materials Needed:

posterboard—40 pieces 2″ × 5″
scissors
felt-tipped pen
paper clips
strip of lightweight wood for fishing pole—12″
string
small magnet

## Making the Game:

Cut the posterboard pieces into the following fish shape.

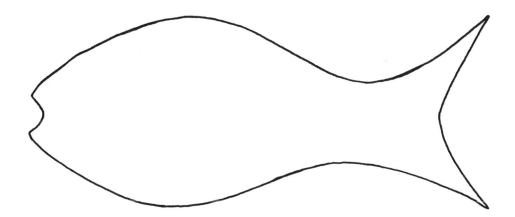

Put one of your current vocabulary words on each fish. Then attach a small paper clip to each one.

Tie one end of the piece of string to one end of the strip of wood, and the other end of the string to the magnet.

71

# Sight Word Knowledge

## Student Game Directions:

1. Spread the fish out on the floor.

2. Have a friend or two play this game with you.

3. Using the fishing pole, pick up a fish. Say the word on the fish. If you say it right, you keep it. If you say it wrong, throw it back in.

4. The person with the most fish at the end of the game is the winner.

# Picture Sentence

*(High Primary–Low Intermediate)*

## Materials Needed:

pictures
posterboard—12 pieces 1″ by length of sentence
                12 pieces 6″ × 6″
glue or tape
felt-tipped pen

## Making the Game:

Glue or dry mount the pictures on the 6″ × 6″ pieces of posterboard.

Now write a short sentence describing each picture. Put them on the 1″ pieces of poster-board.

## Student Game Directions:

1. Spread all the picture cards out on a flat surface. Take a few minutes to look at the pictures and see what is happening in each one.

2. The thin strips contain a sentence that describes a picture.

3. Read a sentence strip and match it with the picture card that it describes.

4. Have someone check your work.

# Apples and Crates

*(High Primary–Intermediate)*

## Materials Needed:

posterboard— 2 pieces 6″ × 11″ (green)
20 pieces 1½″ × 2½″ (yellow)
20 pieces 1½″ × 2″ (red)
scissors
felt-tipped pen

## Making the Game:

Cut out the following truck shape, using the green posterboard pieces.

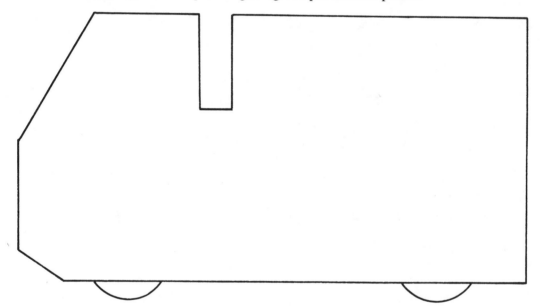

On one side of the yellow pieces draw the following.

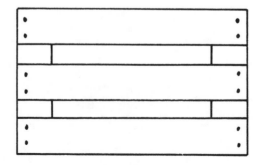

74

On the other side print short sentences appropriate for the ability level of those students with whom you are working.

Cut out apples from the red pieces of posterboard.

On one side of each apple print a word appropriate for the level of your students.

## Student Game Directions:

1. Two people play this game at a time.

2. Each player takes one green truck.

3. Turn the apples and crates face down, so that you cannot see the words or sentences.

4. The object of the game is to load up your truck with as many apples or crates full of apples as you can. Each apple is worth one point while each crate is worth five points. The player at the end of the game with the most points is the winner.

5. Choose someone to go first.

6. Pick either an apple or a crate and turn it over. Read the word or the sentence. If read correctly you may load it on your truck. Continue until all the apples and crates are loaded.

# Word Checkers

*(High Primary–Intermediate)*

## Materials Needed:

posterboard—6 pieces 8″ × 8″
poker chips—8 of one color and 8 of another color
felt-tipped pen

## Making the Game:

Using the six pieces of posterboard, lay out six gameboards similar to the one following. Use a different list of words for each of the boards.

| any | to | it | is | which | one |
|------|--------|-------|-------|-------|-------|
| any | to | it | is | which | one |
| these | there | this | that | tree | today |
| these | there | this | that | tree | today |
| the | with | begin | start | wrong | red |
| the | with | begin | start | wrong | red |
| white | blue | yellow | green | black | brown |
| white | blue | yellow | green | black | brown |
| cow | orange | horse | house | path | road |
| cow | orange | horse | house | path | road |
| see | street | car | cat | can | cold |
| see | street | car | cat | can | cold |

## Student Game Directions:

1. Pick one of the word checkerboards and choose a friend to play this game with you.

2. Each person takes a set of colored chips.

3. In order for a person to move his chips, he must be able to say the word he has landed on. The other person should be listening to make sure the word is said correctly.

4. You may jump your friend's chips just as if you were playing real checkers.

5. The player with most chips of the opposite color is the winner.

# Word Concentration

## *(High Primary–Intermediate)*

## Materials Needed:

posterboard—50 pieces 2″ × 4″
felt-tipped pen

## Making the Game:

Select 25 words that your students are learning. Words may be selected from the basal series or from the Dolch Word List. But the best words are those choosen by the children—their own words!

Print each word on *two* cards.

## Student Game Directions:

1. Two people play this game at a time.

2. Place the cards on a table face down.

3. Choose someone to go first.

4. Pick up two cards. If they match (have the same word) and you can say the word, you keep both cards and continue your turn. When you do not make a match or you cannot say the word, you put the cards back and the other player takes his turn.

5. This continues until all cards have been collected by the players. Each player counts his cards. The person with the most cards wins.

# Alphabetizing
## *(Intermediate)*

## Materials Needed:

posterboard—25 pieces 2″ × 4″ (5 red, 5 blue, 5 green, 5 orange, 5 yellow)
felt-tipped pen

## Making the Game:

Put the following words on the color cards:

| GREEN | RED | ORANGE | YELLOW | BLUE |
|---|---|---|---|---|
| abridge | chemist | barren | resolve | slit |
| loath | cranny | bromine | reproach | slim |
| tension | distract | boom | refuge | slight |
| granite | device | buoy | research | sling |
| hearth | connote | blaze | regret | slip |

## Student Game Directions:

1. Separate the cards according to colors.

2. Take one color at a time and put the cards in alphabetical order.

3. If you have time, arrange the card categories that are alphabetized in the order that they are in the alphabet.

4. Have someone check your work.

# Vocabulary-Punctuation

*(Intermediate)*

## Materials Needed:

posterboard—10 pieces 1″ × 4″ (green)
            10 pieces 1″ × 2″ (red)
felt-tipped pen

## Making the Game:

Put the following words on the 1″ × 4″ pieces of posterboard.

| | |
|---|---|
| parentheses | dots |
| quotation marks | dash |
| colon | apostrophe |
| question mark | semicolon |
| comma | period |

Put the following punctuation marks on the 1″ × 2″ pieces of posterboard.

| | |
|---|---|
| ( ) | . . . |
| " | — |
| : | , |
| ? | ; |
| , | . |

## Student Game Directions:

1. Separate the green cards from the red cards.

2. The green cards contain the names of common punctuation marks that you use when you write sentences.

3. The red cards contain the symbols or punctuation marks you use.

4. Match the name of the punctuation mark with the symbol.

80

# Triangle Twist

## *(Intermediate)*

### Materials Needed:

posterboard— 5 pieces 4″ × 4″ (red)
               15 pieces 4″ × 4″ (yellow)
scissors
felt-tipped pen

### Making the Game:

Cut triangles from the posterboard pieces. Make them about the same size as the following patterns.

Print the following words on the red triangles as shown. Print one definition on each of the yellow triangles. (See the illustrations.)

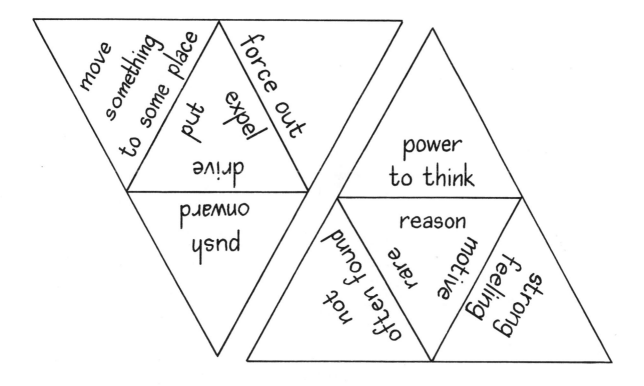

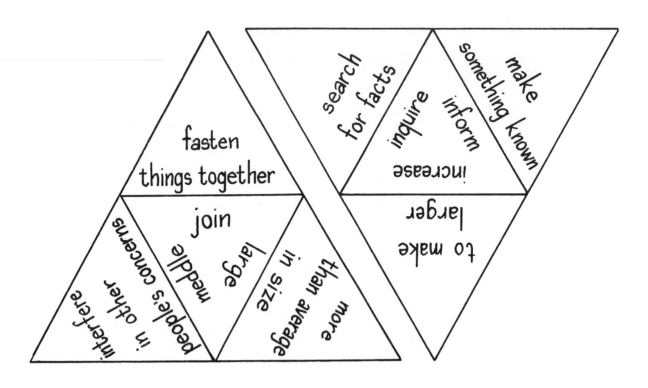

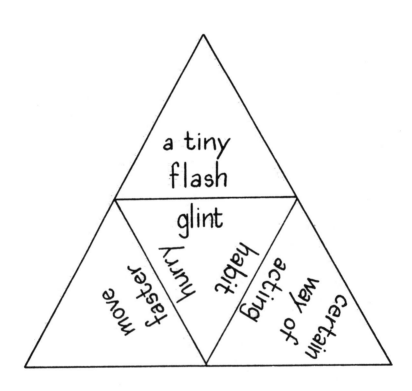

## Student Game Directions:

1. Take a red triangle out of the box and place it face up on your desk.

2. Now place the yellow triangles face up on your desk. Choose one of the words on your red triangle. Find a definition on a yellow triangle that explains what the word means.

3. Place the yellow definition triangle next to the red word triangle as shown below.

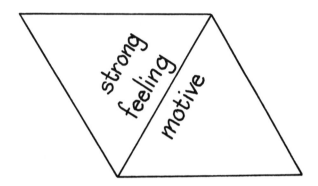

4. Continue this until all of the yellow definition triangles have been matched with the red word triangles.

5. Have someone check your work.

# If You Were. . .

*(High Intermediate)*

## Materials Needed:

posterboard— 6 pieces 2″ × 10″ (red)
                40 pieces 1¼″ by length of word (yellow)
felt-tipped pen

## Making the Game:

Copy the following sentences on the red posterboard pieces.

If you were <u>pretty</u> what words would you think of besides <u>picture</u>?

If you were <u>noisy</u> what words would you think of besides <u>bang</u>?

If you were <u>sad</u> what words would you think of besides <u>cry</u>?

If you were <u>quiet</u> what words would you think of besides <u>whisper</u>?

If you were <u>happy</u> what words would you think of besides <u>smile</u>?

If you were <u>sleepy</u> what words would you think of besides <u>bed</u>?

Copy the following words on the yellow posterboard pieces.

laugh, tickle, loud, blue, horn, yawn, pillow, crash, mirror, tears, beautiful, hurt, snore, silence, chuckle, hush, fun, frown, blanket, rainy, handsome, lovely, graceful, gorgeous, exquisite, murmur, hoot, rumble, roar, unhappy, sorrowful, downcast, depressed, gloomy, miserable, still, noiseless, mute, cheerful, content

## Student Game Directions:

1. Take the red pieces of posterboard out of the box and place them on a flat surface. Put the yellow pieces in a stack.

2. Read one of the sentences on a red card. Now look through the yellow cards and find more words that fit with that sentence. Place them under that red card.

3. Continue through the rest of the cards.

4. Have someone check your work.

# Ladder Likenesses

*(High Intermediate)*

## Materials Needed:

posterboard— 8 pieces 3″ × 7″
                 40 pieces 3″ × ½″
scissors
felt-tipped pen

## Making the Game:

Cut the 3″ × 7″ pieces of posterboard into the following pattern.

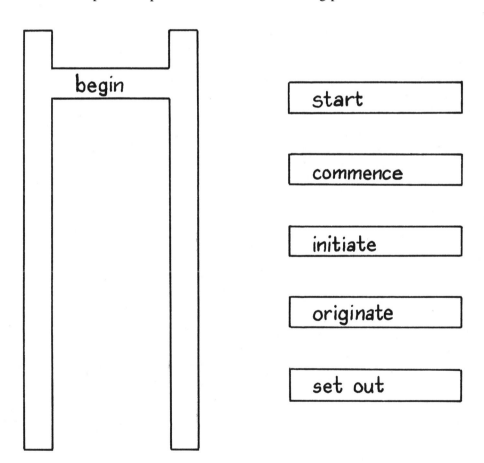

# Sight Word Knowledge

Below are eight groups of six words each that mean nearly the same thing. Put one of these words from each group on the top run of the cut-out ladders. Put the rest of the words on the 3″ × ½″ pieces of posterboard as shown above.

| | | | |
|---|---|---|---|
| different | end | little | begin |
| unequal | close | small | start |
| diverse | terminate | puny | commerce |
| varied | conclusion | tiny | initiate |
| contrasting | finish | miniature | originate |
| divergent | completion | minute | set out |
| | | | |
| large | flat | sharp | slow |
| big | plane | pointed | creep |
| great | even | spiked | lag |
| massive | smooth | acute | linger |
| mighty | flush | spiny | saunter |
| spacious | level | keen | dawdle |

## Student Game Directions:

1. Take out the ladder forms and place them face up on a flat surface.

2. Take out the rungs of the ladders and place them face up on a flat surface.

3. You must match the ladder rungs with the correct ladder form. In order to do this, the word on the rung must mean the same as the word on the top rung of the ladder.

4. Have someone check your work.

# 3 · Phonetic Analysis

The study of English phonology is essential to the reading program. For while our English language is not wholly phonetic, therefore creating the need for sight word knowledge, it is phonetic enough to allow for an association of printed letter-symbols with characteristic speech sounds. It is important that a well-organized sequence be presented to children in the primary reading levels with appropriate reinforcement as reading ability progresses. The following sequential order of phonetic skills is recommended for classroom use.[1]

1. Initial Consonant Phonemes

   /b/, /d/, /f/, /h/, /j/, /k/, /l/, /m/, /n/, /p/, /r/, /t/, /v/, /w/, /y/, /z/

2. Short and Long Vowel Sounds

3. Initial Consonant Blends

   bl, cl, fl, gl, pl, sl
   br, cr, dr, fr, gr, pr, tr
   sc, sk, sm, sn, sp, st, sw, scr, spr, str, spl

4. Irregular Consonants

   C as /s/ and /k/
   X as /ks/ and /z/

   Q as /kw/
   G as /g/ and /j/
   S as /s/, /z/, /zh/ and /sh/

5. Consonant Digraphs

   CH as /ch/, /k/, and /sh/
   SH as in shirt
   TH as in the (voiced)
            thing (voiceless)
   GH as in laugh and ghost
   WH as in what
   PH as in phone

6. Silent Letters

   W as in wrong
   K as in knob
   B as in comb
   C as in sick
   L as in walk
   G as in gnaw
   H as in honest
   T as in witch
   U as in guide
   GH as in light

7. Vowels Followed by R

   Ar as in car
   ER as in her
   IR as in fir
   Or as in for
   UR as in nurse

---

[1]The ordering of the phonetic skill sequence was taken from Iris M. Tiedt and Sidney W. Tiedt, *Contemporary English in the Elementary School* (Englewood Cliffs, N.J.: Prentice-Hall, Inc., 1967), pp. 268-273.

## Phonetic Analysis

8. Vowel Digraphs

AI as in rain
AY as in may
EE as in meet
EA as in easy
OA as in boat
OW as in own
EI as in ceiling
OE as in toe
EY as in key

9. Vowel Diphthongs

OI as in oil
OY as in boy
OW as in cow
OU as in out

Many of the games and activities found in this section may be easily adjusted to reinforce any of a number of these phonetic skill areas.

# Know Your Vowels Game

## *(Low Primary)*

## Materials Needed:

posterboard—1 piece 12″ × 18″
dice
markers to move on the gameboard
felt-tipped pen

## Making the Game:

Put the following on the posterboard in order to make the gameboard.

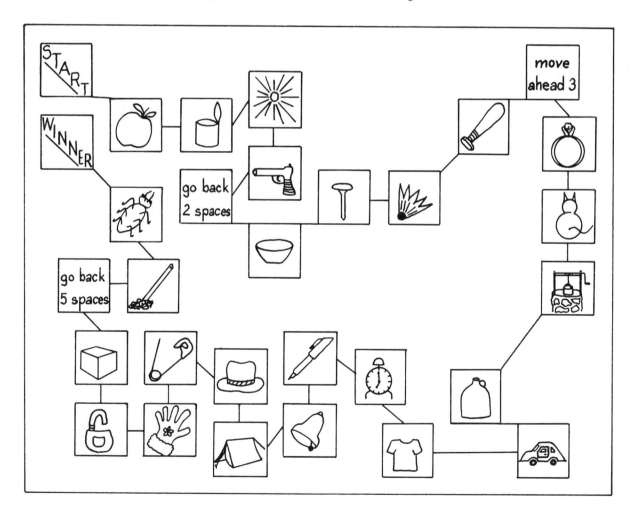

*Phonetic Analysis*

## Student Game Directions:

1. You will need a friend to play this game with you.

2. Place the gameboard on a flat surface.

3. Place the markers on START. Each person rolls the dice to see who goes first (the higher number).

4. Roll the dice and move the amount of spaces it says. Say the name of the item in the space and say one additional word that has the same vowel sound. If you cannot do this or say a wrong vowel sound, you must move back to the space from which you started your move.

5. The first person to reach the space marked WINNER is the winner.

# Sound it Out

*(Low Primary)*

## Materials Needed:

posterboard— 5 pieces 6″ × 9″
                45 pieces 3″ × 3″
ruler
felt-tipped pen

## Making the Game:

Copy the following lines and letters on the 6″ × 9″ pieces of posterboard and the following pictures on the 3″ × 3″ pieces of posterboard.

*(Initial Consonants)*

| L | F | B |
|---|---|---|
| T | C | N |
| D | W | S |

91

# Phonetic Analysis

*(Initial Consonants)*

| B | C | H |
|---|---|---|
| G | F | K |
| P | R | M |

*(Initial Blends)*

| TR | BR | CR |
|----|----|----|
| GR | CL | FL |
| SN | ST | SP |

*(Initial Blends and Digraphs)*

| WH | TH | CH |
|----|----|----|
| SH | GL | SL |
| ST | SP | SN |

| A | E | I |
|---|---|---|
| O | U | A |
| E | I | O |

## Student Game Directions:

1. Take one of the game cards out of the box and place it on your desk.

2. Turn all the picture cards face up.

3. Say the name of the picture. What letter does it begin with?

4. Place the card on the gameboard in the box that begins with the same letter.

5. Have someone check your work.

# Phoneme Match

*(Low Primary)*

## Materials Needed:

posterboard—8 pieces 8″ × 11″
felt-tipped pens (various colors)
scissors
four pairs of 16″ shoelaces (each pair a different color)

## Making the Game:

Copy the following illustrations on the posterboard.

Punch a hole next to each illustration, as shown below.

On the reverse side color the corresponding picture holes the same color. Use felt-tipped pens.

*Initial Consonant Gameboards:*

(W, B, H, hard C)                    (D, F, K, M)

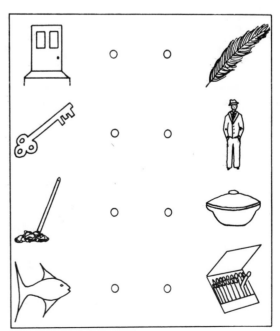

# Phonetic Analysis

*Initial Consonant Gameboards, cont.*

(L, B, N, hard G)

(P, R, S, T)

*Initial Blends:*

(TR, BR, CR, GR)

(GL, CL, SL, FL)

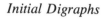

*Initial Blends (con't)*

(SN, SK, SP, ST)

*Initial Digraphs*

(WH, TH, CH, SH)

## Student Game Directions:

1. Take one card and the shoelaces out of the box.

2. Place a shoelace in the hole next to a picture. Say the name of the picture. What sound does it begin with?

3. Now look on the other side of the card. Can you find a picture that begins with the same sound? Put the shoelace through that hole.

4. Do the rest of the card.

5. Turn the card over when you are done. Check to see if your answers are right by seeing if the same shoelace is in two holes having the same color.

# Phonogram (Word Family) Match

*(Low Primary)*

## Materials Needed:

posterboard—3 pieces 8″ × 11″
felt-tipped pens (various colors)
scissors
four pairs of 16″ shoelaces (each pair a different color)

## Making the Game:

Copy the following illustrations on the posterboard. Punch a hole next to each illustration, as shown. On the reverse side color the corresponding picture holes the same color. Use felt-tipped pens.

(ACK, AKE, AP, UG)                    (AIL, AT, AN, AME)

(EST, UNK, ELL, ET)

## Student Game Directions:

1. Take one card and the shoelaces out of the box.

2. Place a shoelace in the hole next to a picture. Say the name of the picture. What sound does it end with?

3. Now look on the other side of the card. Can you find a picture that ends with the same sound? Put the shoelace through that hole.

4. Do the rest of the card.

5. Turn over the card when you are done. Check to see if your answers are right by seeing if the same shoelace is in two holes having the same color.

# Draw the Sound

## *(Low Primary)*

## Materials Needed:

posterboard—1 piece 8″ × 10″
construction paper—3 sheets 8″ × 11″
ruler
felt-tipped pen
scissors

## Making the Game:

Set up a gameboard on the piece of 8″ × 10″ posterboard as shown below. Print consonants on the top of the board and sketch pictures of items beginning with the consonant above in the column below.

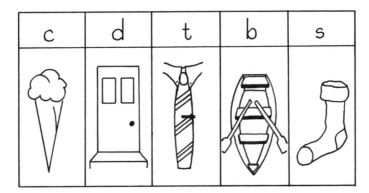

Cut 2″ × 4″ pieces from the construction paper.

## Student Game Directions:

1. Look at the gameboard that has the pictures on it. At the top of the gameboard is the letter that begins each word.

2. Take the construction paper segments and draw your own picture of something that would begin with one of the letters on the top of the gameboard.

3. Do as many as you have time for. Remember: Don't copy a picture already on the gameboard.

4. Show your work to the teacher or a partner.

# Blue Balloon Blends

## *(Low Primary)*

## Materials Needed:

posterboard—2 pieces 8″ × 11″ (blue)
            2 pieces 1½″ × 11″
felt-tipped pen
scissors
glue or tape

## Making the Game:

Print the following blends on one of the posterboard strips. Put the following drawings on the other posterboard strips.

Cut the 8″ × 11″ pieces of posterboard into the balloon shape as shown on page 102. Cut out two windows in one of the balloon pieces as shown. Make them 1″ × ½″. Glue or dry mount the two balloon pieces together at the sides.

## Student Game Directions:

1. Take the balloon out of the box and place the posterboard strips through the balloon. You should see the blends and pictures in the windows.

2. Match the blend with the picture of a word that begins with that blend.

3. Move the picture strip until you find it.

4. Have someone watch as you do it. Say the words.

*Phonetic Analysis*

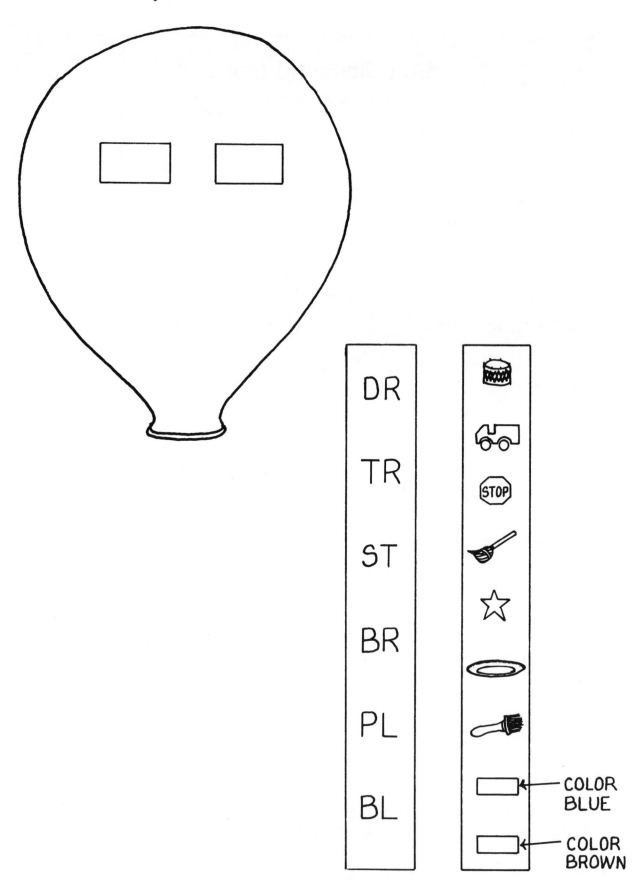

DR

TR

ST

BR

PL

BL

COLOR
BLUE

COLOR
BROWN

# Initial Consonant Blastoff

*(Low Primary)*

## Materials Needed:

posterboard— 1 piece 12″ × 4″
              10 pieces  1″ × 1″
scissors
felt-tipped pen

## Making the Game:

Cut a rocket from the 12″ × 4″ piece of posterboard. Use the following pattern. Print the lower-case consonants in the windows.

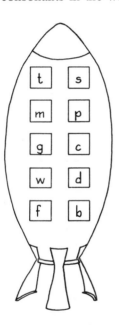

Print both the upper- and lower-case letters on one side of the 1″ × 1″ pieces of posterboard. On the other side of each of these pieces glue or draw a picture that begins with that consonant.

## Student Game Directions:

1. Take the rocket out of the box and place it on a flat surface. Place the small cards next to the rocket with the picture side facing up.

2. Say the name of the picture. What sound does it begin with? Look on the rocket. Can you find the letter-window that the picture begins with? Place the picture card on the letter-window. Continue this until all of the picture cards are on the rocket.

3. Turn them over to see if you are right.

# Be a Star
## *(Low Primary)*

**Materials Needed:**

posterboard—5 pieces 6″ × 6″
scissors
felt-tipped pen

**Making The Game:**

Using the following pattern, cut out star forms from each of the five pieces of posterboard.

Now print the following word families on the various segments of the star.
Example:

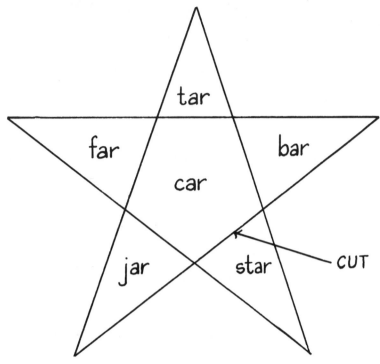

Word Families:

| A | B | C | D | E |
|---|---|---|---|---|
| car | it | at | bet | run |
| star | fit | hat | let | fun |
| jar | bit | bat | get | sun |
| bar | sit | sat | met | bun |
| tar | kit | mat | net | gun |
| far | hit | cat | jet | pun |

Cut the stars apart on the lines as shown above.

## Student Game Directions:

1. Put the parts of the stars on a flat surface with the word side up.

2. Find one of the centers of a star. This has a word on it. It is your job to match the correct star points to this center. The words must end alike, that is, they must be word families.

3. Have someone check your answers.

# Consonant Substitution

## *(Low Primary)*

## Materials Needed:

posterboard— 6 pieces 3″ × 7″
                25 pieces 3″ × 3″
felt-tipped pen
stapler

## Making the Game:

Print the following words on the 3″ × 7″ pieces of posterboard. Also print the following letters on the 3″ × 3″ cards.

| BAN | SAT | NET | TANG | RAKE | PINE |
|-----|-----|-----|------|------|------|
| T   | F   | M   | S    | T    | F    |
| R   | R   | B   | B    | F    | L    |
| C   | B   | S   | R    | B    | D    |
| V   | M   | G   | F    | M    | W    |

Staple the corresponding 3″ × 3″ pieces to the left end of the 3″ × 7″ pieces of posterboard.

## Student Game Directions:

1. Take out one of the cards. Say the word on the card.

2. Now fold back the initial consonant and say the word. What is similar about the words? Fold back the consonant and say the word with a different initial consonant.

3. Try the other cards.

4. Have someone listen as you say the words.

# Begin Alike

*(Low Primary)*

## Materials Needed:

posterboard— 2 pieces 4″ × 7″
                12 pieces 3″ × 5″
felt-tipped pen

## Making the Game:

Print the following phrases on the two large posterboard pieces.

DO NOT BEGIN ALIKE
BEGIN ALIKE

Print the following word lists on the 3″ × 5″ pieces of posterboard.

| | | | | | |
|---|---|---|---|---|---|
| book<br>basket<br>balloon | show<br>shirt<br>shovel | lamp<br>ladder<br>lips | moon<br>mop<br>ring | gate<br>girl<br>bat | cup<br>cake<br>sun |
| dog<br>doll<br>truck | hat<br>hammer<br>house | fan<br>fire<br>fence | wagon<br>watch<br>will | table<br>tulip<br>tiger | man<br>moon<br>noise |

## Student Game Directions:

1. Take the cards that say DO NOT BEGIN ALIKE and BEGIN ALIKE and place them on your desk or another flat surface.

2. Take the cards and place them in a pile in front of you.

3. Look at the words on the card. You may want to say the words aloud. If the words on the card all begin with the same letter, place it in a pile under the card saying BEGIN ALIKE. If they don't all begin with the same letter, place it in a pile under the card saying DO NOT BEGIN ALIKE.

4. Have someone check your work.

# Vowel Pocket Charts
## *(Primary)*

## Materials Needed:

posterboard
pictures
tape or glue
10 envelopes
felt-tipped pen

## Making the Game:

Dry mount or glue the pictures on posterboard.

Print the vowels (long and short) on the envelopes.

## Student Game Directions:

1. Take the picture cards and the envelopes with the vowels on them out of the box.

2. Place the envelopes on a flat surface so that you can see all of them.

3. Take a picture card and say the word of the item in the picture. What vowel sound do you hear? Is it long or short?

4. Place the picture into the pocket that has the correct vowel on it. Try another one.

5. When you are done, have someone check to see if you are right.

# Clown Match

## *(Primary)*

## Materials Needed:

posterboard—2 pieces 8″ × 11″
　　　　　　8 pieces 1½″ × 11″
felt-tipped pen
scissors

## Making the Game:

Print the following words on pairs of the 1½″ × 11″ posterboard strips.

| *Word Families* | | *Vowel Sounds* | |
|---|---|---|---|
| bed | rat | bed | farm |
| mouse | house | car | horn |
| sat | fiddle | her | straw |
| light | ring | form | red |
| bee | red | ball | certain |
| shoe | right | lawn | walk |
| riddle | ice | cool | foot |
| lock | wire | hat | flood |
| dear | car | ride | no |
| nice | tear | we | coat |
| sing | drink | book | moon |
| pear | blue | blood | fat |
| far | tree | go | slide |
| sink | nose | boat | she |
| hose | fear | teach | rock |
| wear | chair | got | man |
| fire | clock | hand | jump |
| | | bug | seat |

# Phonetic Analysis

| Initial Consonants | | Final Consonants | |
|---|---|---|---|
| run | bat | trip | not |
| can | fun | cent | club |
| good | jacks | plum | bag |
| moon | very | grab | pick |
| sat | kill | sad | hill |
| took | happy | if | map |
| been | could | dog | glad |
| dig | doll | back | calf |
| jump | like | call | ran |
| we | ride | can | room |
| net | got | stop | door |
| look | sun | clear | likes |
| fan | till | bus | runs |
| hide | place | his | fast |
| keep | nice | which | both |
| pool | man | fish | cash |
| vine | wise | tenth | pitch |
| | | must | cap |

Cut the following clown shape from the two large pieces of posterboard.

Cut out the eye spaces in one of the pieces of posterboard. Dry mount or glue the two pieces together at the ears.

## Student Game Directions:

1. Take the clown head out of the box and place the strips down through the head. You should see the words in his eyes.

2. Match the words that have something in common. On the back of each strip is written the skill of the game. Be sure you have two strips with the same skill on the back.

3. You will find one word on each strip. Move the strip until you find it.

4. Have someone watch as you do it. Say the two words.

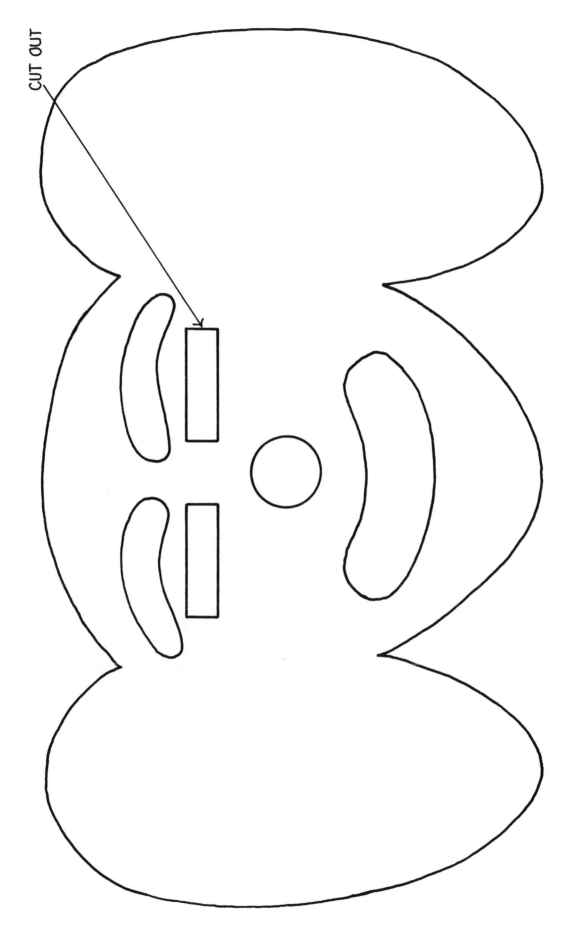

CUT OUT

# Form a Straight Line Game

## *(Primary)*

## Materials Needed:

posterboard— 3 pieces 8″ × 8″
                 48 pieces 2″ × 2″
ruler
felt-tipped pen

## Making the Game:

Print the following letters on the three gameboards as shown below.

| Bb | Ff | Kk | Dd |
|----|----|----|----|
| Hh | Gg | Cc | Rr |
| Ww | Ll | Pp | Tt |
| Jj | Nn | Ss | Mm |

| Cc | Pp | Gg | Ss |
|----|----|----|----|
| Dd | Mm | Hh | Nn |
| Jj | Bb | Kk | Rr |
| Ff | Ww | Tt | Ll |

| Gg | Bb | Jj | Ll |
|----|----|----|----|
| Nn | Cc | Rr | Mm |
| Kk | Pp | Ff | Ww |
| Hh | Dd | Tt | Ss |

Put the following drawings on the 2″ × 2″ pieces of posterboard.

# Phonetic Analysis

## Student Game Directions:

1. Choose a partner to play this game.

2. Each player is to choose a gameboard.

3. Place all of the picture cards face down on a flat surface.

4. Decide who begins. The first player turns over one of the picture cards. He says the word and places it on the appropriate initial consonant. The next player does likewise. This continues. If a player makes a mistake, he misses a turn.

5. The winner of this game is the first player who forms a straight line of four squares. It may be vertical, horizontal, or diagonal.

# Final "E" Fold

*(Primary)*

## Materials Needed:

posterboard—28 pieces 3″ × 5½″
ruler
felt-tipped pen

## Making the Game:

Fold the right end of the posterboard over 1″ as shown.

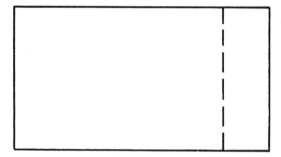

Print the letter E on each of the folds.

Now print the following words on the posterboard as shown.

rid, rat, pin, cut, tot, bit, mat, cap, plan, mad, kit, sit, hat, hid, past, pal, strip, fat, bath, rip, tap, twin, quit, fin, win, dim, can, pan

# *Phonetic Analysis*

## Student Game Directions:

1. Place the pieces of posterboard with words on them flat on your desk.

2. Take the first one and say the word. Does the vowel in the word have a long or short sound?

3. Now fold the posterboard so that you can see the "e".

4. Say the word after you have added the "e". What sound does the vowel have now?

5. Have a partner listen to you to see if you have said the words right. Let him try it and you listen to him.

# Puzzle Blends

## *(Primary)*

## Materials Needed:

posterboard—26 pieces 2″ × 4″ (yellow)
26 pieces 2″ × 4″ (green)
felt-tipped pen

## Making the Game:

Print the following blends on the yellow pieces of posterboard.

bl, cl, fl, gl, pl, sl, br, cr, dr, tr, fr, gr, st, sp, str, sm, sn, sc, pr, scr, spr, thr, sk, sw

Print the following word endings on the green pieces of posterboard.

ue, own, ower, ove, an, ap, own, y, ain, ap, ill, ain, reet, rain, ap, all, ail, are, ay, eam, ain, ow, ate, im

## Student Game Directions:

1. Separate the cards having blends (yellow cards) from those with the other letters on them (green cards).

2. You must make a match with a blend and the proper word endings.

3. After you have made a match, say the word. If it sounds funny, you may not have made a word.

4. You may make more than one word using the same endings and different blends.

5. Have someone check your work.

# Consonant Game

*(Primary)*

## Materials Needed:

posterboard—15 pieces 2″ × 3″ (yellow)
15 pieces 2″ × 2″ (green)
felt-tipped pen

## Making the Game:

Print the following consonants on the green cards.

s, b, b, c, f, f, c, d, s, s, r, r, l, s, f, f

Print the following word endings on the yellow cards.

at, ee, un, ee, aw, og, un, aw, at, og, an, at, un, an, at

## Student Game Directions:

1. Separate the cards with consonants on them from the cards that have two letters on them—the yellow cards from the green cards.

2. Which consonant would you add to the card with two letters on it to make a complete word?

3. Find the consonant and make the word. You might find more than one consonant that will fit.

4. Have a partner play the game with you and see how many words you can make together.

5. Make sure someone can check your work.

# Initial Consonant Ladder

*(Primary)*

## Materials Needed:

posterboard— 6 pieces 2″ × 4″ (orange)
               38 pieces 2″ × 4″ (green)
felt-tipped pen

## Making the Game:

Print the following words on the orange cards.

take, line, bat, bet, sang, can

Print the following words on the green cards.

ban, pan, van, Dan, man, fan, ran, tan, make, cake, bake, fake, rake, lake, wine, pine, fine, dine, mine, nine, fat, sat, mat, hat, rat, cat, Nat, set, wet, met, get, jet, let, hang, rang, gang, bang, fang.

## Student Game Directions:

1. Take the orange cards out and spread them out on a flat surface.

2. Taking one green card at a time, place each one under the orange card that has the same word ending.

3. You are making word families.

4. Have someone check your work.

# Phonics Wheel

*(Primary)*

## Materials Needed:

posterboard—2 circles 8″ diameter
2 circles 4″ diameter
felt-tipped pen
scissors
2 round-headed paper fasteners

## Making the Game:

Print the following letters on the outside edge of the 4″ circles:

BA   CA

Print the following letters on the outside edge of the 8″ circles:

| | |
|---|---|
| R | MP |
| G | P |
| T | RD |
| LL | SH |
| NG | N |
| IT | R |
| SE | D |
| CK | ST |

Punch holes through the centers of all four circles. Fasten each of the small circles to one of the larger circles with a paper fastener.

## Student Game Directions:

1. Take out one of the phonics wheels.

2. Each time you turn the center wheel you make a new word.

3. Turn the wheel to a letter or letters. Say the word. Now move it to the next set of letters and do the same thing.

4. Have someone play with you and take turns as each of you says the words.

# Oh! No! Game

## *(Primary)*

## Materials Needed:

posterboard—21 pieces 2″ × 4″
felt-tipped pen

## Making the Game:

Print the following words on the pieces of posterboard.

fall, height, hill, bite, free, bee, hat, see, bat, fight, ball, fill, sat, hall, sight, stall, still, he, bill, fat, OH! NO!

## Student Game Directions:

1. To play this game you must have three players.

2. Divide all the cards between the players.

3. The object of the game is to make pairs of words. To make a pair, the words must sound alike, like rhyming words.

4. Choose someone to go first. This person may select a card from the other player without seeing the card faces. If you make a pair, you may lay the cards down face up. It is now the other person's turn.

5. You must also try to get rid of the card that says OH! NO!

6. The first person to pair up all his cards and not have the OH! NO! card is the winner. You cannot win, even though you have laid down all your cards, if you have the OH! NO! card.

# Say or Pay

*(High Primary)*

## Materials Needed:

posterboard— 3 pieces 10″ × 10″
                         20 pieces  2″ × 2″
ruler
felt-tipped pen

## Making the Game:

Print an equal number of 1's and 2's on the 2″ × 2″ cards.

Print the following on the gameboards.

| spr | skip | that | out | cow | move ahead 2 |
|-----|------|------|-----|-----|--------------|
| go back 2 | | | | | jump |
| fry | | SAY | | | the |
| yes | | OR | | | wh |
| sh | | PAY | | | bl |
| START | WINNER | ch | talk | dog | go back 2 |

| plan | miss a turn | scr | chin | fl | go back 3 |
|------|-------------|-----|------|-----|-----------|
| cl | | | | | br |
| in | | SAY | | | cup |
| go ahead 2 | | OR | | | tr |
| mother | | PAY | | | fall |
| START | WINNER | hall | th | hill | go back 4 |

122

| coin | oil | house | miss a turn | short | joy |
|------|-----|-------|-------------|-------|-----|
| mouse | | | | | go back 5 |
| ahead 1 | | SAY | | | toy |
| owl | | OR | | | noise |
| cow | | PAY | | | plow |
| START | WINNER | brow | loud | boy | join |

## Student Game Directions:

1. Take out one gameboard. No more than two people can play this game at one time.

2. Place your marker on START. Pick up a number card and move as many spaces as it says. If you land on a word, you must say it if you want to move on the next turn.

3. Place the number tags face down in the center of the gameboard.

4. If you land on a blend or digraph, you must say the sound the letters make and then say a word that begins with those letters.

5. Your friend should listen as you say the words. If you make a mistake, you must either lose a turn or return to START.

6. You must follow all other directions on the playing board if you land on them. The first one around the gameboard is the winner.

# Missing Vowels

## *(High Primary)*

## Materials Needed:

posterboard— 5 pieces 2″ by the length of the sentences
50 pieces ½″ × 2″
felt-tipped pen

## Making the Game:

Copy the following sentences on the pieces of posterboard:

Th_ d_g kn_w m_ny tr_cks.
Th_ b_ys _nd g_rls h_d f_n _t th_ p_rty.
Th_ h__t _f th_ s_mm_r w_s t_rn_ng th_ l__v_s br_wn.
_t w_s f_n sw_mm_ng _n th_ p__l.
M_nk_ys sw_ng _n tr__s by _s_ng th__r t__ls.

Copy the following vowels on the ½″ × 2″ pieces of posterboard.

e, o, e, a, i, e, o, a, i, a, u, a, e, a, e, e, a, o, e, u, e, a, u, i, e, e, a, e, o, i, a, u,
i, i, i, e, o, o, o, e, i, i, e, e, u, i, e, i, a, i.

## Student Game Directions:

1. Place the long strips with sentences on them on the desk.

2. Look at the incomplete words in the sentence and decide which vowels would complete each word correctly.

3. Take the strips with vowels on them and place the correct ones in the blank spots of the words.

4. Have a friend check your work.

# Rain Puddles

## *(High Primary)*

## Materials Needed:

posterboard— 5 pieces 7″ × 11″ (blue)
              20 pieces 2″ ×  3″
scissors
felt-tipped pen

## Making the Game:

Cut out puddles from the 7″ × 11″ pieces of posterboard. Print the following on the puddles.

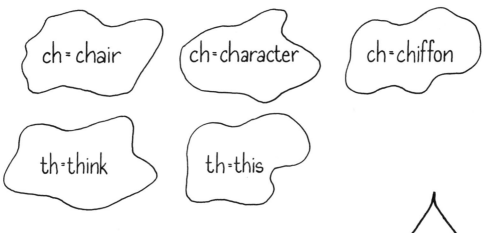

Cut out raindrops from the 2″ × 3″ pieces of posterboard.

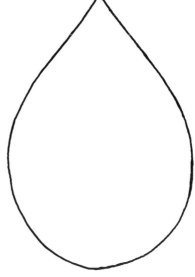

# Phonetic Analysis

Print the following words on these raindrops, one per raindrop.

| | | | |
|---|---|---|---|
| chop | child | chorus | chord |
| cheat | choose | chemist | chrome |
| chef | chic | chamois | chauffeur |
| thing | thimble | that | they |
| thank | third | those | though |

## Student Game Directions:

1. Place the puddles face up on your desk.

2. Take a raindrop and place it on the puddle that has a word that begins with the same sound as the word on the raindrop.

3. Continue until all of the raindrops have been placed on the puddles.

4. Turn the raindrops over to see if you are correct. The number on the back of the raindrop should be the same as the number on the puddle.

# 4 · Structural Analysis

When a youngster attempts to decode an unfamiliar word, the child relies not only upon phonetic skills to aid him, but also upon the structure of the word. Certainly, the knowledge of the prefix "un" would be essential in order to derive correct meaning of the word "unimportant." And knowledge of breaking a word into syllables is necessary when attempting to pronounce words of two or more syllables.

The games and activities within this section are devised to help reinforce the following structural analysis skills.

Prefixes
Suffixes
Compound Words
Contractions
Syllabication

# Finding the Plurals

*(Primary)*

## Materials Needed:

posterboard— 4 pieces 8″ × 8″
     32 pieces 1″ × 2″
ruler
felt-tipped pen

## Making the Game:

Make the following gameboards on the 8″ × 8″ pieces of posterboard.

| | | |
|---|---|---|
| car | | |
| lunch | | |
| fox | | |
| fly | | |
| glass | | |
| peach | | |
| army | | |
| boy | | |

Do not lift until game is over

| | | |
|---|---|---|
| tree | | |
| bird | | |
| dress | | |
| inch | | |
| puppy | | |
| splash | | |
| period | | |
| school | | |

Do not lift until game is over

| house | | | Do not |
|-------|---|---|--------|
| penny | | | lift until |
| candy | | | |
| baby | | | game is |
| couch | | | over |
| kiss | | | |
| paint | | | |
| class | | | |

| flash | | | Do not |
|-------|---|---|--------|
| city | | | lift until |
| desk | | | |
| book | | | game is |
| brush | | | over |
| bench | | | |
| cry | | | |
| girl | | | |

Print the following plural suffixes on the 1″ × 2″ pieces of posterboard.

9—s
14—es
8—ies

## Student Game Directions:

1. Take one of the large playing boards out of the box. Be sure that the flap is folded over so that you can see, "Do Not Lift Until Game Is Over."

2. Read the first word. Now make this word mean more than one by adding a plural suffix. Select a correct suffix located on the small posterboard pieces and place it next to the base word.

3. Continue down the list of words.

4. When you are finished, lift up the flap and correct yourself.

# Suffix Paragraph

*(High Primary)*

## Materials Needed:

posterboard— 1 piece 8″ × 12″

10 pieces 2″ × 2″

felt-tipped pen

## Making the Game:

Copy the following paragraph on the large sheet of posterboard.

> Tom and Joe want__ to go fish__. They pick__ up their pole__ and bait can__ and walk__ to their favorite stream. The sun was beam__ down when they start__, but by the time they began to fish, the sky began cloud__ over. It soon began rain__ and the two boy__ ran for cover.

Put the following suffixes on the small cards.

ed;    ing;    ed;    s;    s;    ed;    ing;    ed;    ing;    ing;    s

## Student Game Directions:

1. A suffix is a word ending.

2. Read the paragraph. Some of the words are missing suffixes.

3. Read the paragraph again, this time adding the suffix cards to the ends of the words that need them.

4. Read the paragraph a third time to see if you are correct.

5. Have someone check your work.

# Suffix Builders

## *(High Primary)*

## Materials Needed:

posterboard—33 pieces 2″ × 5″ (white)
           12 pieces 2″ × 5″ (red)
felt-tipped pen

## Making the Game:

Copy the following root words on the red pieces of posterboard:

| | | |
|---|---|---|
| work | jump | buy |
| whisper | go | read |
| call | walk | bring |
| want | yell | wish |

Copy the following words on the white pieces of posterboard.

| | | |
|---|---|---|
| worked | working | workable |
| jumps | jumper | jumping |
| jumped | buying | buyer |
| whispered | whispering | going |
| goes | reading | reader |
| reads | readable | calling |
| calls | called | walking |
| walked | brings | bringing |
| wants | wanting | wanted |
| yelled | yelling | wished |
| wishful | wishes | wishing |

## Student Game Directions:

1. Pick out all the cards containing root words (on red cards) and place them out on a flat surface.

2. You must build a ladder using these root words by placing the cards having the root word and a suffix ending under it. There will be several cards in each suffix ladder.

3. Read the cards in the ladders. How has the meaning of the root word changed with the various suffix endings?

4. When you have finished turn the cards over. If you have grouped the words correctly, the numbers in each group will be identical.

# Contraction Paragraph

*(High Primary–Low Intermediate)*

## Materials Needed:

posterboard— piece 8″ × 12″
            13 pieces 1″ × 2″
felt-tipped pen

## Making the Game:

Put the following paragraph on the large posterboard. Leave a 3″ space for each contraction.

> Today is the birthday party. All the children _____ arrived yet, but I _____ think it will take much longer. I just _____ wait for it to begin so _____ all play the games. I _____ played pin-the-tail on the donkey since . . . I _____ remember when. Last year I _____ have a party so there _____ as much fun as _____ have today. Joan is coming and _____ bet that _____ bring the best present. But I _____ care what I get, _____ all have a good time.

Put the following contractions on the small cards.

> haven't, didn't, we'll, don't, wasn't, don't, we'll, I'll, haven't, she'll, can't, don't, we'll

## Student Game Directions:

1. Read the paragraph without filling in words for the blank spaces.

2. Go through the paragraph again, this time placing contraction cards in the blank spaces.

3. Read the paragraph again. Does it make sense?

4. Have someone read your paragraph.

# Division of Syllables

*(High Primary–Low Intermediate)*

## Materials Needed:

posterboard—20 pieces 2″ × 6″ (white)
　　　　　　　45 pieces ¼″ × 2½″ (blue)
felt-tipped pen

## Making the Game:

Put words of varying numbers of syllables on the 2″ × 6″ pieces.

## Student Game Directions:

1. Place all the word cards in one pile.

2. Say the word on the first card. How many syllables does it contain? Where should the word be divided?

3. Taking the blue strips of paper, place them between the letters in the word that would separate the syllables.

4. Have someone check your work.

# Syllabication Flip

*(High Primary–Low Intermediate)*

## Materials Needed:

posterboard—5 pieces 8″ × 10″
5 pieces 3″ × 3″
5 round-headed metal paper fasteners
ruler
scissors
felt-tipped pen

## Making The Game:

Fold and cut one of the 8″ × 10″ pieces as shown in the following illustration.

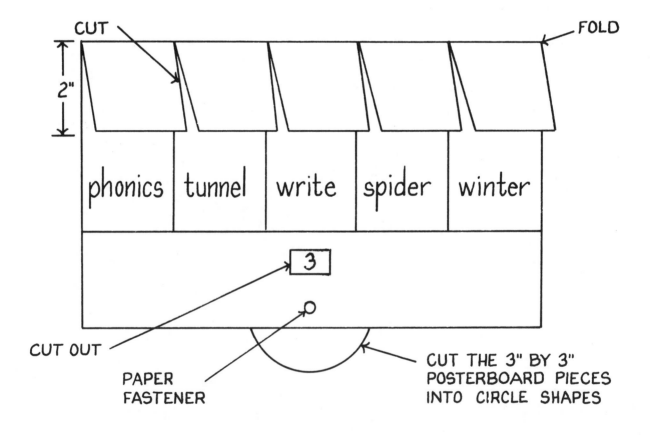

Prepare the other four 8″ × 10″ pieces of posterboard in the same manner but using the following words:

| A | B | C | D |
|---|---|---|---|
| candy | moment | summer | tumble |
| locomotive | formation | detective | tiger |
| situation | education | slippery | release |
| unhappily | exporter | expandable | disloyalty |
| removable | rearrangement | submerged | impassable |

## Student Game Directions:

1. Take out one gameboard. Be sure all the flaps are folded down.

2. Look at the first word. Say it. How many syllables does it have? Turn the wheel until this number appears in the window.

3. Lift the flap in order to check yourself. Continue across the gameboard.

# Compound Match

*(High Primary–Low Intermediate)*

## Materials Needed:

posterboard— 6 pieces 8″ × 8″
                     48 pieces 1″ × 2″
ruler
felt-tipped pen

## Making the Game:

Make the following gameboards using two of the 8″ × 8″ pieces of posterboard. Each word in the left-hand column is the first half of a compound word.

| | | Do not lift until game is over |
|---|---|---|
| any | | |
| some | | |
| when | | |
| him | | |
| snow | | |
| wind | | |
| tooth | | |
| motor | | |

| | | Do not lift until game is over |
|---|---|---|
| broad | | |
| air | | |
| any | | |
| ever | | |
| after | | |
| air | | |
| sand | | |
| her | | |

To complete the gameboards, lift up the flap on the right-hand side and write the complete compound word in the appropriate column.

Prepare four more gameboards in a similar manner using the following words in the left-hand column.

| | | | |
|---|---|---|---|
| rail | sales | life | eye |
| book | life | north | pig |
| horse | light | down | class |
| light | country | finger | slow |
| up | pepper | short | black |
| with | grass | house | note |
| birth | flag | flood | high |
| basket | peace | other | blow |

Print the following words on the 1″ × 2″ pieces of posterboard. (These are the second half of compound words.)

| | | | |
|---|---|---|---|
| was | noon | man | stop |
| thing | port | time | boat |
| ever | box | house | light |
| self | self | side | wise |
| man | road | mint | ball |
| shield | case | hopper | tail |
| brush | shoe | pole | mate |
| cycle | house | time | poke |
| cast | set | jacket | smile |
| craft | out | west | smith |
| one | day | power | book |
| green | ball | tip | power |
| | | | out |

## Student Game Directions:

1. Take one of the large playing boards out of the box. Be sure that the flap is folded over so that you can see "Do Not Lift Until Game Is Over."

2. Read the first word. Now look through the small pieces of posterboard for another word that will form a compound word when placed next to the first one.

3. Continue down the list of words.

4. When you are finished, lift up the flap and correct yourself.

# Prefix Match

## *(High Primary–Intermediate)*

## Materials Needed:

posterboard—36 pieces 2″ × 5″ (white)
          7 pieces 2″ × 2″ (red)
felt-tipped pen

## Making the Game:

Put the following words on the 2″ × 5″ pieces of posterboard.

| | | |
|---|---|---|
| correct | sure | accurate |
| continue | clean | polite |
| appoint | agree | patient |
| possible | certain | willing |
| safe | color | use |
| charge | complete | direct |
| visible | human | formation |
| traction | claim | victim |
| mark | cover | call |
| strain | appoint | agree |
| arm | arrange | place |
| figure | occupation | |

Put the following prefixes on the 2″ × 2″ pieces of posterboard.

in, im, dis, un, re, pre, con

## Student Game Directions:

1. Take the red cards out of the box. Each red card has a prefix on it. A prefix is a set of letters appearing at the beginning of a word that changes the meaning of the word.

2. Set the red prefix cards down on a flat surface, with the letters facing up.

3. Take the white cards out of the box. Each one has a word on it.

4. Now match the white word cards with the correct prefix cards. There may be more than one word that can be matched with the same prefix. Place the words under the correct prefix cards.

5. Have someone check your work.

# Suffix Match

*(High Primary–Intermediate)*

## Materials Needed:

posterboard—28 pieces 2″ × 4″
felt-tipped pen

## Making the Game:

Put the following words on 14 cards.

| | | |
|---|---|---|
| near | use | care |
| encourage | wait | suit |
| magic | disappear | assist |
| legend | wood | sorrow |
| man | express | |

Put the following suffixes on 14 cards.

| | | |
|---|---|---|
| less | ment | ly |
| ful | ing | able |
| al | ance | ant |
| ary | en | ful |
| hood | ion | |

On the reverse sides of the matched pairs put identical numbers.

## Student Game Directions:

1. From your study of what a suffix is, you should find this game easy.

2. You must match a word with a proper suffix ending. (For example, if a card has the word "use" on it you might match it with a card having the ending "ful.")

3. When you are finished, turn over the matching pairs of cards and check yourself. The numbers will be the same if you are correct.

# Suffix Strips

*(High Primary–Intermediate)*

## Materials Needed:

posterboard—10 pieces 2½″ × 7″
                  10 pieces 3″ × 8″
scissors
felt-tipped pen

## Making the Game:

Cut two slits in the 2½″ × 7″ pieces as shown. Put words and suffixes on the cards as follows.

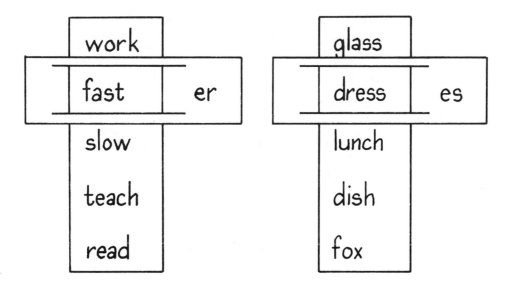

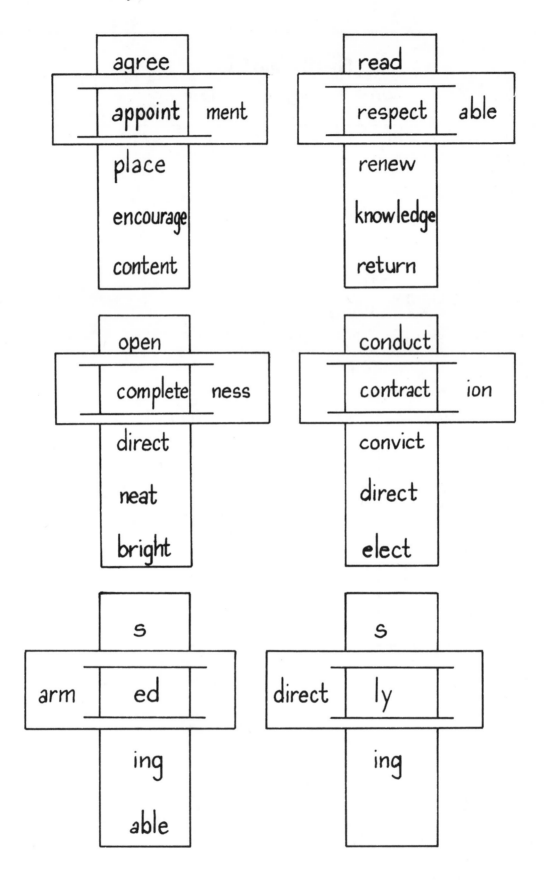

agree
appoint | ment
place
encourage
content

read
respect | able
renew
knowledge
return

open
complete | ness
direct
neat
bright

conduct
contract | ion
convict
direct
elect

s
arm | ed
ing
able

s
direct | ly
ing

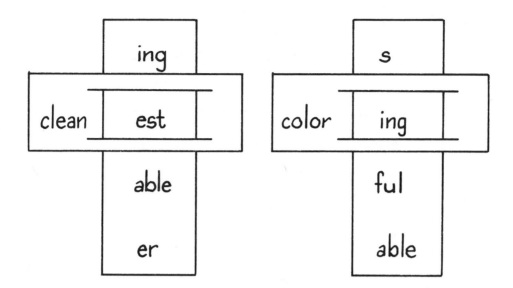

## Student Game Directions:

1. There are four different types of cards in this box. Separate them as follows: A card with a suffix ending on it goes with a card with words on it. A card with a single word on it goes with a card with several suffix endings.

2. In each case, you must say the word before you add the suffix. Now say it with the suffix. How has the meaning of the word changed? Slide the card down to the next word or suffix ending, depending on which one you are working on.

# Compound Puzzle

*(High Primary–Intermediate)*

## Materials Needed:

posterboard—2 pieces 8″ × 10″
felt-tipped pen
scissors
shoestring—ten pairs (16″)

## Making the Game:

Put the following words on the 8″ × 10″ pieces of posterboard. Punch holes next to the words.

*Primary Gameboard*

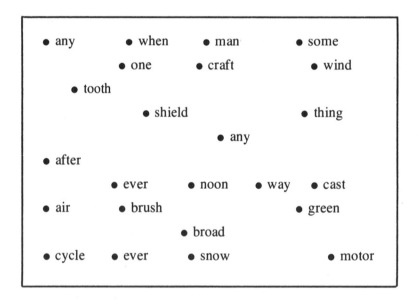

*Intermediate Gameboard*

| | | | | | |
|---|---|---|---|---|---|
| • man | • side | • poke | • light | • time | |
| • boat | • life | • wise | • mint | • slow | |
| • country | • flag | • eye | • north | • jacket | |
| • grass | • down | • short | • tip | • house | |
| • hopper | • west | • flood | • ball | • other | • life |
| • time | • finger | • class | • peace | • light | |
| • pole | • pour | • sales | • pepper | • stop | • mate |

## Student Game Directions:

1. Take the gameboard and the shoelaces out of the box.

2. Choose one of the words on the board and thread a shoelace through the hole to the left of that word.

3. Now look over the board and try to find another word that will combine with the first word to make a compound word. When you have found it, thread the other end of that shoelace into the hole to the left of the second word.

4. Continue until you have matched all of the words forming compound words.

# Compound Word Puzzle

## *(High Primary–Intermediate)*

## Materials Needed:

posterboard—30 pieces 3″ × 8″
felt-tipped pen
scissors

## Making the Game:

Put the following compound words on the cards. Then cut the two words in the compound word apart in a variety of cuts so that no two cuts are the same. You may use the following patterns.

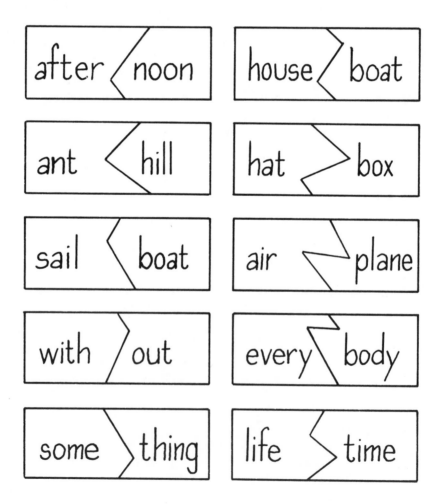

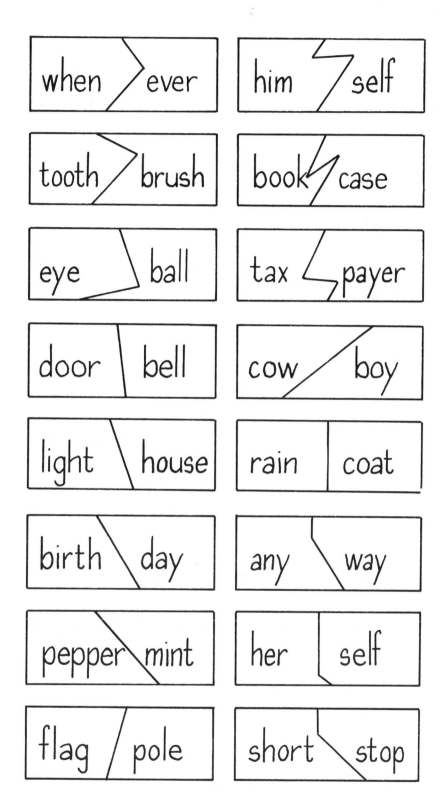

when | ever
him | self
tooth | brush
book | case
eye | ball
tax | payer
door | bell
cow | boy
light | house
rain | coat
birth | day
any | way
pepper | mint
her | self
flag | pole
short | stop

*Structural Analysis*

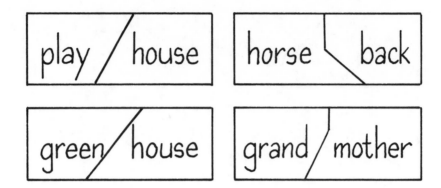

## Student Game Directions:

1. There are many compound words in the box. You must match the correct combinations together.

2. A compound word will be two words that will match perfectly. Each word has been cut a certain way. If it doesn't fit when placed together, you have not made a compound word.

# Compound Cupboard

*(High Primary–Intermediate)*

## Materials Needed:

posterboard—6 pieces 3″ × 12″
pictures from magazines or readiness book
ruler
tape or glue
felt-tipped pen

## Making the Game:

Fold each posterboard strip as shown in the accompanying illustration:

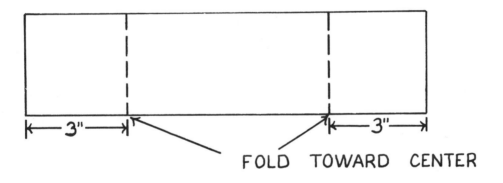

Select two pictures that give clues to the parts of a compound word, for example, pictures of an arm and of a chair, for ''armchair.'' Then dry mount or glue the pictures on *top* of the folds of a posterboard strip.

Write the compound word itself under the folds to provide a quick self-check.

| *Suggested Words:* | pan | cake | mail | man |
| --- | --- | --- | --- | --- |
| | doll | house | door | frame |
| | dish | washer | arm | chair |

(Check the Appendix for additional compound words.)

# Structural Analysis

## Student Game Directions:

1. *Do not* unfold the posterboard strips.

2. Each picture means one word, but when put together forms a compound word.

3. Write your answer on a sheet of paper.

# Syllabication Flash

*(High Primary–Intermediate)*

## Materials Needed:

posterboard—20 pieces 2″ × 5″
felt-tipped pen

## Making the Game:

Put the following words on the pieces of posterboard.

| | | |
|---|---|---|
| bullet | picture | interest |
| inside | prescribe | discolor |
| mother | station | reclaim |
| able | pencil | happy |
| table | ladies | invisible |
| recent | beside | machine |
| mountain | car | |

Now put the correct number of syllables on the reverse side of each card.

## Student Game Directions:

1. Play this game in a small group of two or three people or by yourself.

2. Say the word on the card. How many syllables do you hear when you say the word? If you are playing by yourself, you can check yourself by looking at the back of the card.

3. If you are playing in a group, the person who has the most cards wins the game.

# Contraction Match

*(High Primary–Intermediate)*

## Materials Needed:

posterboard—60 pieces 2″ × 4″
felt-tipped pen

## Making the Game:

Put the following contractions on 30 pieces of the posterboard.

| | | |
|---|---|---|
| they've | I'll | you'd |
| weren't | aren't | they'll |
| haven't | let's | doesn't |
| that's | couldn't | you're |
| didn't | isn't | we've |
| shouldn't | there's | you've |
| can't | they'd | we're |
| we'd | he's | we'll |
| hadn't | what's | he'll |
| won't | it's | she'd |
| she'll | wasn't | you'll |
| don't | they're | hadn't |
| I'm | hasn't | |

Put the following words on 30 pieces of the posterboard.

| | | |
|---|---|---|
| they have | I will | you would |
| were not | are not | they will |
| have not | let us | does not |
| that is | could not | you are |
| did not | is not | we have |
| should not | there is | you have |
| cannot | they did | we are |
| we would | he is | we will |
| had not | what is | he will |
| will not | it is | she would |
| she will | was not | you will |
| do not | they are | had not |
| I am | has not | |

## Student Game Directions:

1. The cards in this box contain words that are contractions and the two words that a contraction is made up of.

2. First separate the words into two piles; one with contractions and one with the rest of the words.

3. Either play with a partner or by yourself. You must say the card that contains two words and then find the card with its matching contraction.

4. When you are finished, turn over the matching pairs of cards and check yourself. The numbers will be the same if you are correct.

# Compound Octagons
*(High Primary–Intermediate)*

## Materials Needed:

posterboard—4 pieces 8″ × 8″
              4 pieces 4″ × 4″
scissors
felt-tipped pen

## Making the Game:

Cut off the corners of all the pieces of posterboard in order to make octagons. Place the small pieces in the center of the large ones and outline with the pen.

Now copy the following compound words on the pieces. (Check the Appendix for additional compound words.)

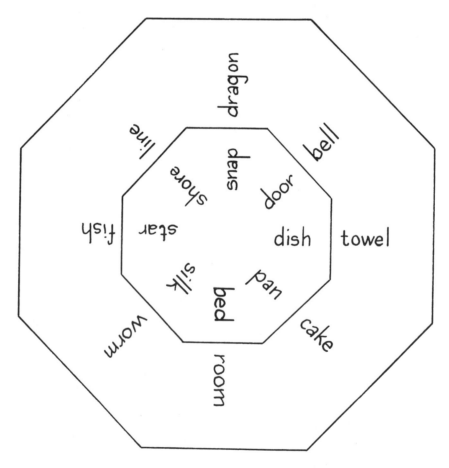

## Student Game Directions:

1. Take the large cards and place them face up on your desk. These cards contain the last half of eight compound words.

2. Now take one of the small cards and place it face up on your desk. This card contains the first half of eight compound words.

3. Place it on the center of one of the large cards. Do the words make sense? If not, turn it or place it on another large card until all the words form eight compound words.

# Flip-to-Move Game

*(Intermediate)*

## Materials Needed:

posterboard— 1 piece 10″ × 16″
             25 pieces  2″ × 2½″ (green)
markers to move in the game
felt-tipped pen

## Making the Game:

Make the following gameboard:

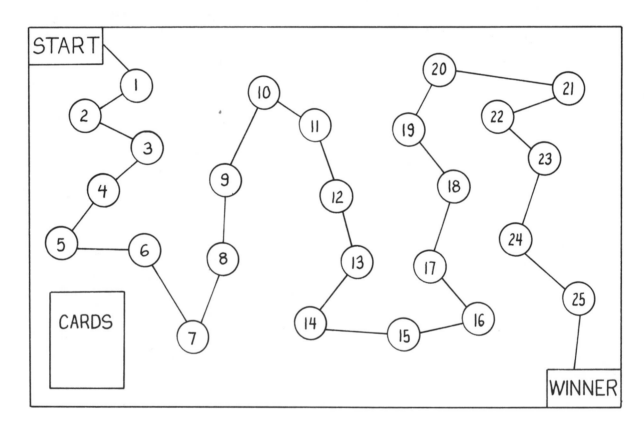

Copy the following on the 2″ × 2½″ cards.

> How many syllables in—APPLE (1 move)
> How many syllables in PHILOSOPHY (2 moves)
> Divide into syllables—AKNUT (1 move)
> Divide into syllables—AROCLE (2 moves)
> Which syllable is accented—SAILBOAT (1 move)
> Divide into syllables—BRITAS (1 move)
> Divide into syllables—EKON (1 move)
> Divide into syllables—KEJKEY (3 moves)
> Which syllable is accented—CHICKEN (1 move)
> Add the suffix ER to GOST (2 moves)
> Add the suffix ING to SOGPEPE (2 moves)
> Divide into syllables—BIRAS (2 moves)
> How many syllables in—HAPPINESS (1 move)
> Which syllable is accented—LONELY (1 move)
> Add the prefix UN to HAPPY (1 move)
> How many syllables in—RATE (1 move)
> Which syllable is accented—ACCIDENTAL (1 move)
> Add the prefix DIS to REGARD (1 move)
> Add the suffix ED to NES (2 moves)
> Which syllable is accented—UNIVERSAL (1 move)
> Which syllable is accented—COPPER (1 move)
> Add the prefix EX to CHANGE (1 move)
> Divide into syllables—SILNAP (1 move)
> Add the suffix EST to CLY (2 moves)

## Student Game Directions:

1. Two people play this game at a time.

2. Place the green cards in the space marked CARDS.

3. Place the markers on START. Choose someone to go first.

4. Pick a card and answer the question. If you are right, move the number of spaces the card says. The first person to reach FINISH is the winner.

# Puzzler

*(Intermediate)*

## Materials Needed:

posterboard— 1 pieces 10″ × 16″
            27 pieces 2″ × 2½″
markers to move in the game
felt-tipped pen

## Making the Game:

Put the following on the large piece of posterboard.

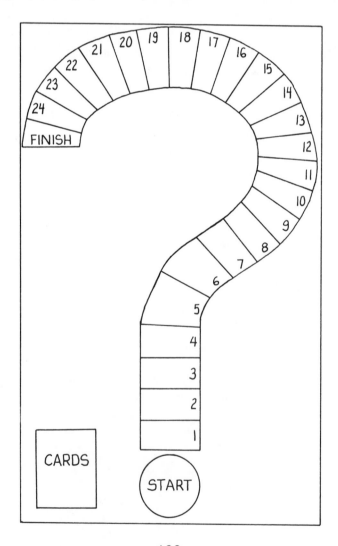

Copy the following on the 2″ × 2½″ cards.

How does the accent change when you add a suffix TION to CONFIRM? (2 moves)

Go to the next card. If your answer is correct, move an extra space.

Where is the accent in the word CONTENT, meaning to be happy with? (2 moves)

Move ahead two spaces.

Go back five spaces.

When dividing a word that contains a digraph, you divide the word within the digraph. True or False? (3 moves)

How many syllables are there in STERILE? (1 move)

Divide PACKAGE into syllables. (1 move)

Where is the accent in the word PRESENT, meaning a gift? (1 move)

Divide MICROSCOPIC into syllables. (2 moves)

When you add ED to TRY, does the base word change? (1 move)

Add ING to OCCUR. (1 move)

How many syllables are there in RETRACTABLE? (1 move)

Where is the accent found in the word SAILBOAT? (1 move)

Which of the following are not diphthongs? OY, OI, OU, TH, OE, OW, CH, OA (3 moves)

Move ahead four spaces.

Go to the next card. If your answer is correct, move 1 extra space. If it is wrong, go back two.

Add the suffix ES to MAKE. (1 move)

Divide these words into syllables: AUTHOR and PENCIL (3 moves)

Add the suffix ING to HOPE. (2 moves)

Add the prefix UN and the suffix ABLE to BELIEVE. (2 moves)

How many syllables are there in REGARDLESS? (1 move)

Go back three spaces.

Divide NONSENSE into syllables. (1 move)

Which syllable is accented in REFRESHMENT? (2 moves)

# Structural Analysis

## Student Game Directions:

1. Two people play this game at a time.

2. Place the cards in the space marked CARDS.

3. Place the markers on START. Choose someone to go first.

4. Pick a card and answer the question. If you are right, move the number of spaces the card says. The first person to reach FINISH is the winner.

# 5 · Comprehension

If excessive time is spent on word analysis skills at the expense of the comprehension skills, youngsters will become "word callers." That is, they are able to decode words and read them one by one without deriving meaning from either singular words or word phrases. It is the assumption of the author that word calling alone should not be considered reading. A child must understand what is read before it can truly be said that he has a reading ability.

Comprehension may be subdivided into various skill groups. The comprehension skills to be found within this section are:

Finding the Main Idea
Reading for Details
Following the Sequence of Events
Determining Cause and Effect
Drawing Conclusions
Following Directions

# Sequence of Events

*(Low Primary)*

## Materials Needed:

posterboard— 5 pieces 4″ × 12″
15 pieces 3″ × 3″ (red)
scissors
felt-tipped pen

## Making the Game:

Cut five 1's, 2's, and 3's from the red posterboard.

Draw the following illustrations on the 4″ × 12″ pieces of posterboard.

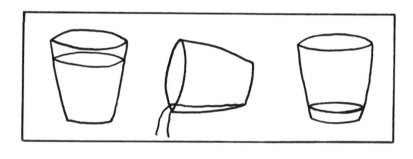

# Comprehension

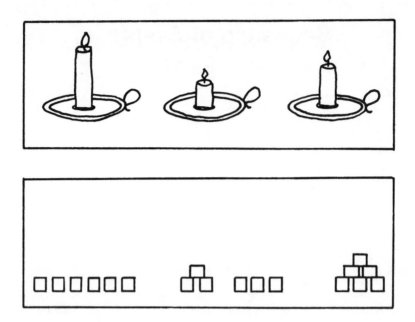

## Student Game Directions:

1. Look at one picture card at a time. There are three pictures on each card but they might not be in the right order.

2. Take the numbers 1, 2, and 3 and place them on the pictures in the correct order.

3. Have someone check your work.

# Sentence Understanding

## *(Primary)*

## Materials Needed:

posterboard—2 pieces 8″ × 12″
              8 pieces 1″ × 1″
felt-tipped pen

## Making the Game:

Put the following on the large pieces of posterboard. Put the numbers 1 through 4 on the small pieces of posterboard.

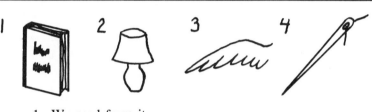

1. We read from it. _____

2. It helps birds fly. _____

3. Mother uses it to sew with. _____

4. It gives us light. _____

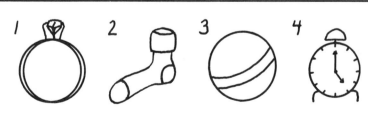

1. You put it on your foot. _____

2. You can bounce it. _____

3. Put it on your finger. _____

4. It wakes you up in the morning. _____

# Comprehension

## Student Game Directions:

1. Take out one of the large cards.

2. Look at the pictures on the card first and decide what they are.

3. Now read all the sentences.

4. Go back to the first sentence and decide what picture is the answer to the statement. In the blank provided, place the card having the same number on it as the picture you have chosen. Do the rest.

5. Have someone check your work.

# Main Idea Match

*(Primary–Intermediate)*

## Materials Needed:

posterboard—10 pieces 7″ × 7″
               10 pieces 6″ × 6″
scissors
tape
felt-tipped pen

## Making the Game:

From an appropriate basal reader, cut out pages that contain both an illustration and part of a story.

Cut these apart and dry mount the pictures on the larger sheets of posterboard and the stories on the 6″ × 6″ pieces.

## Student Game Directions:

1. Separate the picture cards from the story cards.

2. Spread the picture cards out so that you can see all of them.

3. Pick a story card and read it.

4. Which picture shows what is being described in the picture? After you have picked the correct picture, place the story below it in the card holder.

5. Finish the rest.

6. Have someone check your work when you are done.

# Picture Sentence

*(Primary–Intermediate)*

## Materials Needed:

posterboard—10 pieces 1″ by the length of the sentence
                    pictures from magazines/or basal series (10)
tape or glue
felt-tipped pen

## Making the Game:

Dry mount or glue the illustrations on posterboard.

Write a descriptive sentence of each picture on the 1″ posterboard. For example:

A train is crossing a bridge.

## Student Game Directions:

1. Spread out all the picture cards on a flat surface. Take a few minutes to look at the pictures and see what is happening in each one.

2. The thin strips contain a sentence that describes a picture.

3. Read a sentence strip and match it with the picture card that it describes.

4. Have someone check your work.

# Flip-flop Puzzle

*(Primary–Intermediate)*

## Materials Needed:

a picture puzzle with no more than 100 pieces
   (It must be interlocking.)
felt-tipped pen

## Making the Game:

On the back of the puzzle write a story or simply copy a story from an appropriate basal reader.

## Student Game Directions:

1. Find a flat area where you can work on your puzzle.

2. Put the puzzle together, matching the picture segments.

3. Flip the puzzle over carefully when you have finished the puzzle.

4. Read the story on the back, which tells about the picture.

# Sentence Building

## *(Primary–Intermediate)*

## Materials Needed:

posterboard—the number depends upon the number of words in the sentences
  2″ by the length of the word
  (As many different colors as sentences)
felt-tipped pen

## Making the Game:

Copy sentences from basal readers for your appropriate grade level. Each should be on a different color of posterboard. For example:

| Jack | went | fishing | at | the | lake. |

The following sentences may be used according to the ability of the student.

*Primer*

Come and help me.
Now look at me.
See what I can do.
Will you put my hat away?

*First*

This is the man who cuts my hair.
I don't know what that is.
We did not see him come out.
We will come to the zoo next spring.

*Second*

The park has some of the biggest trees that I have ever seen.
He looked until he had found out what he wanted to know.
Something very little came buzzing around the chicken's legs.
Suddenly the swan met a little girl coming along the zoo path.

*Third*

The bike didn't squeak a bit when Bill rode it up the street.

One of them disappeared into a taxicab that was waiting at the corner.

Then out of the darkness came Nancy on her pony Prince.

Johnny could see the brightly painted fishing boats tied up at the shore.

*Fourth*

And then from the sand bar one gull shrieked.

The principal, who wore glasses, sat behind a big desk.

When the world was young and new, people thought everything should be young and new.

When the Indians first settled on the reservation, they lived in tents and hunted wild animals.

*Fifth*

Eventually, people in several tribes would get together for the purpose of carrying on peaceful trade.

Winners of exhibits at county fairs often competed with winners from all over the state.

The announcer began calling the names of the teams that would be competing.

Suddenly Charles began to dance around the room like a man gone crazy.

*Sixth*

Twenty-five contestants started, but a number of them had to drop out along the route.

There was nothing to the Icile except a light, flat frame of basswood, and her sharp, skatelike runners.

Derry shook her head, and her face was a deep, angry red.

As the arctic terns fly south, they cross the Atlantic and travel down the coasts of Europe and Africa.

## Student Game Directions:

1. Separate the different colored cards. Each color makes a different sentence.

2. Arrange the words so that you make a complete sentence.

3. Have someone check your sentences when you are done.

# Cartoon Sequence

*(Primary–Intermediate)*

## Materials Needed:

cartoon strips from a Sunday newspaper
tape or glue
scissors

## Making the Game:

Dry mount or glue the cartoon strips to posterboard. Cut the segments apart.

## Student Game Directions:

1. Lay all of the cartoon segments on a flat surface.

2. Read each of the segments and place them in an order so that the story makes sense.

3. Have someone check your story.

# Comprehension Booklets

*(Primary–Intermediate)*

## Materials Needed:

old basal readers
scissors
construction paper
stapler
felt-tipped pen

## Making the Game:

Break the binding of the basals and tear out stories suitable for your students. Trim the edges and staple in a booklet fashion, using the construction paper as a cover.

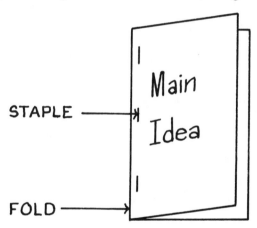

Put the skill on the front of the cover and the ability level in the lower right corner.

On the inside of the back cover write out questions that will reinforce the skill you want to emphasize. The following are merely examples. You must formulate your own questions to correlate with the story.

*Main Idea*

> Can you think of another title for this story?
> The most important idea in this story is . . .
>> that time goes quickly when you are having a good time.
>> that mighty oak trees once were tiny acorns.
>> that honesty is the best policy.
> What do the first two paragraphs tell us about the Halloween parade? Did Nick want to join the parade?

175

# Comprehension

*Details*

Which ship did Columbus sail on . . .
    the Nina,
    the Pinta, or
    the Santa Maria?
Does John live on the same street as Dave?
What animals did Sue and Sara see at the zoo?

*Sequence*

List, on a sheet of paper, in order, the steps that Joe took to purify the water from the old well.

When the story started, how did Chris discover the forest fire? What did he immediately do?

During the trip through the West, Jim and Mike experienced many problems. Think back through their trip and list these difficulties in the order that they happened.

*Cause and Effect*

What caused Columbus to discover America?
In what way did the flat tire on father's car cause a problem for Hilda?
Why did the early settlers travel to the West in wagon trains?

| time | place | characters | event |
|------|-------|------------|-------|
|      |       |            |       |
|      |       |            |       |
|      |       |            |       |

## Student Game Directions:

1. Take one of the reading booklets out of the box.

2. Read it and answer the questions on the back cover.

# Nuts and Bolts Comprehension

*(Primary–Intermediate)*

## Materials Needed:

posterboard—10 pieces 6″ × 6″ (yellow)
             10 pieces 6″ × 9″ (orange)
sentences from graded basal readers
scissors
felt-tipped pen

## Making the Game:

Cut out bolts from the 6″ × 9″ pieces of yellow posterboard using the pattern at the end of this lesson.

Cut out nuts from the 6″ × 6″ pieces of orange posterboard also using the pattern given on page 179.

Print the first part (up to the slash mark) of the following sentences on the bolts. Print the last part (after the slash mark) on the nuts. Turn them over and place the same numeral on each pair.

Use the list of sentences most appropriate for the student with whom you will be using this game.

*Primer*

> Please don't let / the train go.
> I can't get / on the train.
> Take this / and don't let go.
> Here we all go / to the car.

*First*

> I know where / to look for him.
> Here is / your friend Pete.
> We did not / see him come out.
> He began / to jump up and down.

*Second*

> Soon she came home / from school with an animal book.

# Comprehension

See what some of your friends / left in our yard.
I'll put them / with the other lost things.
There's a lot of wind / this morning.

### Third

The wolves eyed the man / and the dog hungrily and began to circle them.
The Indian soon uncovered / a few scattered grains of corn.
Just hold the end / of the ruler.
In the open door he stopped / for a good long look at his latest invention.

### Fourth

So Terry went farther and farther / into the salt ponds.
I had to pass that bear / to get home.
He didn't believe it / when I told him my name.
The principal wasn't / laughing at him.

### Fifth

In each World's Fair that followed / exciting new inventions and discoveries were brought to the attention of the visitors.
It was one of those days / when she felt as if she could do anything.
Bobby hated to see his mother / looking so sad.
When I was your age / this whole valley was filled with ponds and lakes.

### Sixth

Uncle Ed built / a number of camps on Beaver Pond.
The guests knew / they could count on a story.
It was somewhat disappointing to the Greeks / to have an athlete from so far away capture the marathon.
We owe much to our friends around the world / for the thousands of words that we speak each day.

## Student Game Directions:

1. Place the nuts face up on your desk.

2. Select one bolt and read the sentence.

3. Find the nut that best completes the sentence.

4. Place the bolt in the nut.

5. Continue selecting bolts and finding the appropriate nut for each one.

6. When you have finished, turn the nuts and bolts over and check your answers by seeing if the numbers on the back are the same.

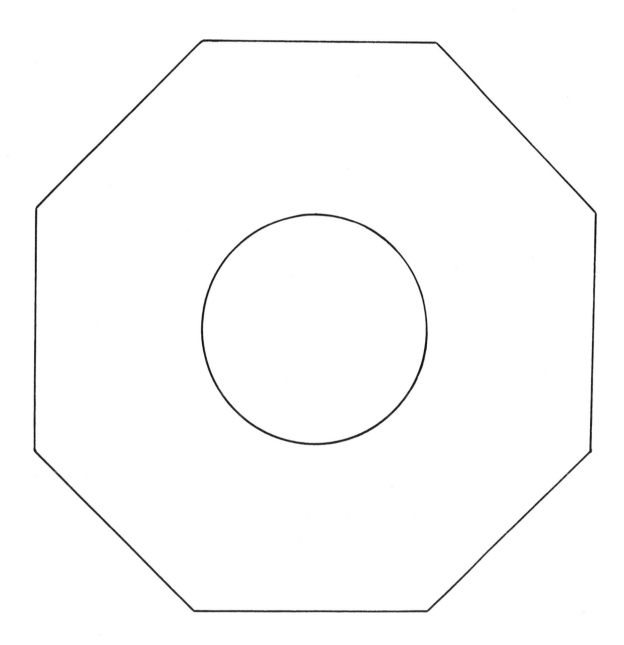

# Comprehension Octagon

*(Primary–Intermediate)*

## Materials Needed:

posterboard—4 pieces 8″ × 8″
　　　　　　4 pieces 4″ × 4″
scissors
felt-tipped pen

## Making the Game:

Cut off the corners of all the pieces of posterboard in order to make octagons. Place the small pieces in the center of the large ones and outline with a fine tip pen.

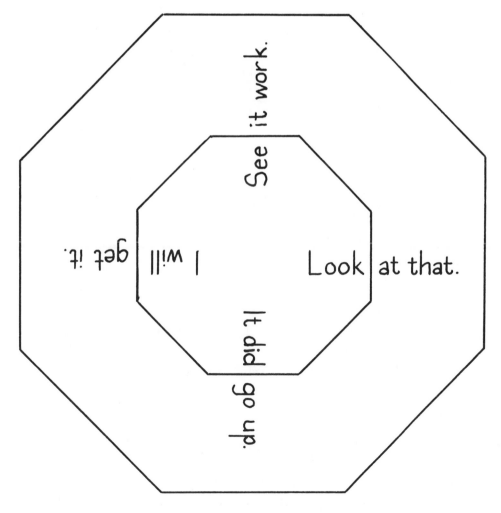

# Comprehension

Now copy the following sentences on the pieces, *or* use other sentences more suited to your students. Listed below are four sample sentences per grade ability level. The slash mark indicates where to divide the sentences.

*Preprimer*

> Look / at that.
> It did / go up.
> See / it work.
> I will / get it.

*Primer*

> Look / at me.
> Come and / help me.
> We have / work to do.
> Can you / do it?

*First*

> I wish I / could be up very late.
> Every night / a pony came galloping along the road.
> I think / I can make your toy.
> Grandfather / ran into the bedroom.

*Second*

> In the barnyard / something big jumped down from the fence.
> "I'm not afraid," / said Yellow Chicken.
> At last / something has scared you!
> You should see / the old farmhouse.

*Third*

> Spring had / turned to summer and summer to fall.
> Squanto was sent / to invite a neighboring Indian chief and his braves.
> He put / the telescope up to his eye.
> There were / lots of people vacationing at Gray Lake this summer.

*Fourth*

> Terry knew that / this was his chance to escape.
> It wouldn't / be so bad while he was standing there.
> Tom had / found the area most interesting.
> And what if / they do not live to enjoy those riches?

*Fifth*

As time went on / villages became larger and larger cities were built.
The first World's Fair / was held in London in 1851.
Once the competition began / Babe realized that she had a difficult task ahead of her.
By now / Pepe was expecting things to be strange.

*Sixth*

Almost at once / the little door opened and the skunks marched in.
Why don't you / invite those men who doubt you to the house?
Most of our / knowledge of bird migration has been gained from bird-banding studies.
Sam climbed up / on a large boulder and stepped across to a teetering block of ice six feet wide.

## Student Game Directions:

1. Take the large cards and place them face up on your desk. These cards contain the last half of eight sentences.

2. Now take one of the small cards and place it face up on your desk. This card contains the first half of eight sentences.

3. Place it on the center of one of the large cards. Do the sentences make sense? If not, turn it or place it on another large card until you have eight complete sentences.

# Unfinished Stories

*(Primary–Intermediate)*

## Materials Needed:

old basal readers
scissors
stapler or glue
construction paper
felt-tipped pen

## Making the Game:

Break the binding of the basals and tear out the beginning of several stories that are suitable for your students. Trim the edges and staple or glue in a booklet fashion, using the construction paper as a cover.

Put the ability level in the lower right corner of the cover.

## Student Game Directions:

1. Take one of the booklets out of the box.

2. Open it and read the beginning of the story.

3. On a piece of paper, finish the story.

# Catch an Ending

*(High Primary–Intermediate)*

## Materials Needed:

posterboard—2 pieces 9″ × 7″
               2 pieces 5″ × 7″
scissors
ruler
glue or tape
felt-tipped pen

## Making the Game:

Cut the 5″ × 7″ pieces as shown. Fold the flaps using a ruler or straight edge so that they fold evenly.

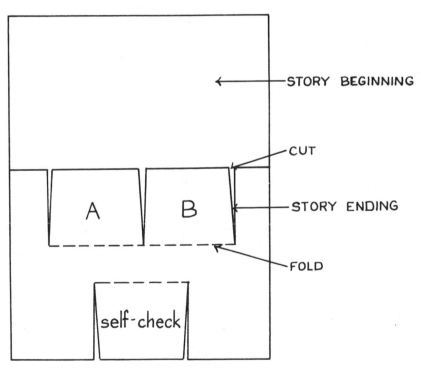

Glue or dry mount the 5″ × 7″ piece of posterboard on top of the large piece. It should be at the bottom as shown above. *Do not* glue the flaps.

Copy the following stories, one each, on the large posterboard pieces as shown above. Don't forget to put the correct answer (A or B) under the self-check flap.

# Comprehension

### Story Beginning

The trip to St Louis was to be an exciting experience for the Clayton family. After all, it isn't every day that you get a chance to attend the opening of a World's Fair. Peter and his sisters were so thrilled that it was almost impossible for them to sit still in their train coach. Mr. Clayton had to keep reminding the children not to be bobbing up and down in their seats all of the time.

### Story Endings:

(A) The boys had so much to see that they could hardly wait to tell mother and father about it. The day had certainly been both fun and exciting. But when they finally arrived home they were both too tired to do anything except to go straight to sleep.

(B) What a day it had been! Sue could not remember when she had seen such wonderful sights. The entire family had enjoyed themselves, but now the long train ride home seemed a good place to sleep and dream of the exciting fair.

### Story Beginning:

If you follow the path through the haunted forest and continue up the jagged mountain, you would come to the castle where the giant lives. His castle is dark and gloomy with one monstrous tower that looks down upon the nearby village of Cataput.

### Story Endings:

(A) How happy the villagers were when Jack came down from the mountain. He was carried and cheered throughout the village and was soon nicknamed, "Jack the Giant-Killer." No longer would the villagers have to live in fear of the mean giant.

(B) How happy the villagers were when the prince returned with his bride. Bells were rung from every part of the kingdom and an official holiday was declared. This was to be the most royal wedding ever to take place in the village of Cataput.

## Student Game Directions:

1. Take one of the gameboards out of the box.

2. Read the story beginning.

3. Lift flap A. Read this story ending.

4. Lift flap B. Read this story ending.

5. Which story conclusion do you think fits best with the story beginning at the top of the gameboard?

6. Check your answer by lifting the self-check flap.

# Cause and Effect Match

*(High Primary–Intermediate)*

## Materials Needed:

posterboard—6 pieces of 2″ by various lengths according to length of sentences (red)

6 pieces of 2″ by various lengths according to length of sentences (green)

felt-tipped pen

## Making the Game:

Copy the following sentences on the red posterboard pieces.

The car ran over a nail.
It has been raining a lot.
The children studied hard for the test.
The wind blew hard last night.
They forgot to wipe their feet on the mat.
The movie is over.

Copy the following sentences on the green posterboard pieces.

The tire is flat.
The river is very high.
Many children received high grades.
Several trees are down.
The floor is all muddy.
People are leaving the theater.

## Student Game Directions:

1. Separate the cards into two piles. The green cards are the effect cards and the red cards are the cause of the effect.

2. Pick an effect card and find the cause of the effect.

3. After you have matched all the cards, have someone check your work.

# Paragraph Sequence

*(High Primary–Intermediate)*

## Materials Needed:

posterboard—6″ width but varying lengths according to each paragraph (a variety of posterboard colors)
felt-tipped pen

## Making the Game:

Using a story from an appropriate basal reader, write each paragraph on a separate piece of posterboard. Each story should be on different color posterboard.

## Student Game Directions:

1. Separate the cards according to color.

2. Take one set of cards.

3. Read the cards. You must place them in the correct order so that the story makes sense.

4. Re-read your story after you have put the cards in order to make sure you have not made any mistakes.

5. Have someone check your work when you have finished all the stories.

# Poetry—Title

*(High Primary–Intermediate)*

## Materials Needed:

poems from old basal readers
tape or glue
scissors

## Making the Game:

Dry mount or glue the poems on posterboard.
Cut the title off of each poem.

## Student Game Directions:

1. Separate the title cards from the poems.

2. Spread the titles out on your desk so that you can see all of them.

3. Read a poem.

4. Look at the title cards. Which one should be the title of the poem you just read? Pick the one you think matches the poem.

5. Read the rest of the poems and do the same thing.

6. Have someone check your work when you are finished.

# Evergreen Comprehension

*(Intermediate)*

## Materials Needed:

posterboard—11 pieces 4″ × 4″ (green)
felt-tipped pen

## Making the Game:

Place the cards on a table in the following position. Print the sentences shown here, or others more suited to your students, on the cards in the following manner.

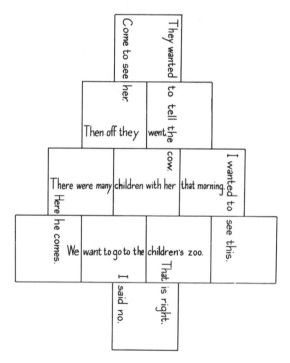

## Student Game Directions:

1. Place the posterboard pieces face up on your desk.

2. Notice that each square of posterboard has at least one partial sentence on it. Find the other part or parts to that sentence and fit them together. Continue this until you have finished with all the pieces.

3. If you are correct, you should have a design that looks like an evergreen tree.

# Rocket Comprehension

*(Intermediate)*

## Materials Needed:

posterboard—8 pieces 4″ × 4″
scissors
felt-tipped pen

## Making the Game:

Cut diagonally across two of the square pieces of posterboard.

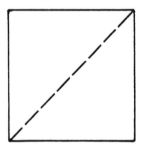

Now place the cards on a table in the position shown in the illustration. Print the following sentences, or others more suited to your students' ability, on the cards in the following manner. (See illustration)

## Student Game Directions:

1. Place the posterboard pieces face up on your desk.

2. Notice that each piece of posterboard has at least one partial sentence on it. Find the other part or parts to that sentence and fit them together. Continue this until you have finished with all the pieces.

3. If you are correct, you should have a design that looks like a rocket.

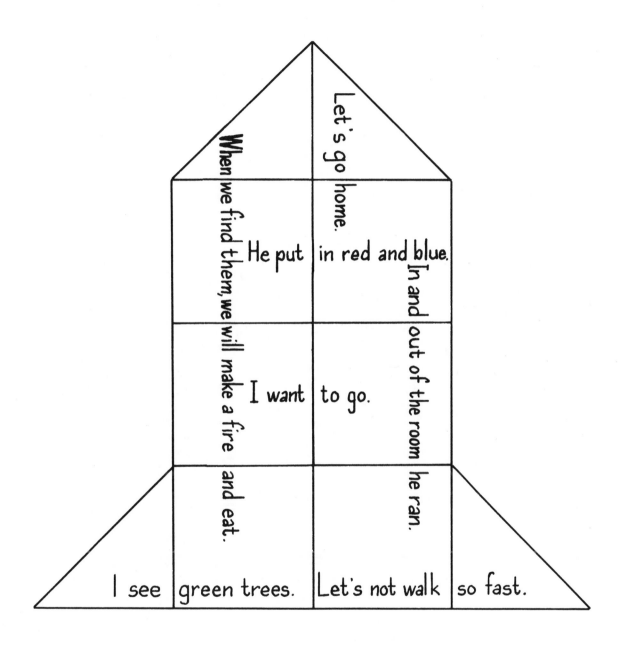

# Because . . .
## *(Intermediate)*

## Materials Needed:

posterboard—4 pieces 6½″ × 9″
            4 pieces 6″ × 6″
scissors
round-headed metal paper fasteners (4)
felt-tipped pen

## Making the Game:

Cut the 6″ × 6″ pieces of posterboard into circles with 6″ diameters.

Attach the circles to the 6½″ × 9″ pieces of posterboard with the paper fasteners. Then cut a window in the large piece of posterboard.

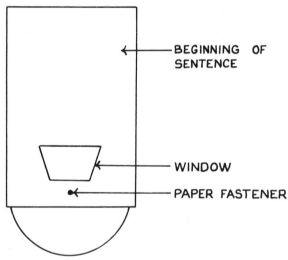

Copy the following sentence beginnings on the top half of the 6½″ × 9″ posterboard pieces. Also copy the corresponding sentence endings on the circles so that they can be read through the window.

*Sentence Beginnings:*

Because Sam's father had been a prospector and had led a very unsettled life,

*Sentence Endings:*

he wanted his son to have a more permanent way of life.

Comprehension

Sentence Beginnings:                    Sentence Endings:

                                        he was so cold during the nineteen-
                                        course dinner that he couldn't enjoy
                                        it.

                                        Mr. Scott almost lost his life.

Because Pa was going to make a          he had to dig a well so that Ma could
trip to town,                           have water while he was gone.

                                        it was impossible to name the one per-
                                        son who played the most beautiful
                                        music.

                                        the construction of the Denver and
                                        Rio Grande Railroad was expensive.

Because he made a dangerous trip        Sam was given a job working for the
and proved he was trustworthy,          railroad.

                                        the train ride from Durango to
                                        Silverton is a popular tourist
                                        attraction.

                                        it was impossible to name the one per-
                                        son who played the most beautiful
                                        music.

Because Japan often had earthquakes     it was necessary to build a building
that did great damage,                  that would float on a sea of mud.

                                        he wanted his son to have a more
                                        permanent way of life.

                                        the men always sent down a candle
                                        into the well first.

## Student Game Directions:

1. Take one of the gameboards out of the box.

2. Read the first half of the sentence that is on the top of the gameboard.

3. Now turn the wheel until a second half of a sentence appears in the window.

4. Read it. Does it make sense when you put it with the first half of the sentence? If not,
   turn the wheel until another second half of a sentence appears in the window. Continue
   until you think the sentence makes sense.

5. Have someone check your gameboards.

# Remember the Order

*(Intermediate)*

## Materials Needed:

posterboard—1 piece 10″ × 14″
              4 pieces 1½″ × 8½″
ruler
scissors
felt-tipped pen

## Making the Game:

Fold over the large piece of posterboard. Cut 1½″ slits as shown below. Slide the poster-board strips in the slits.

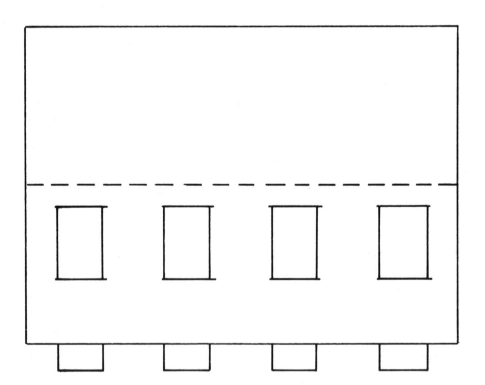

Put the following on the front of the gameboard.

It wasn't so long ago that the idea of exploring outer space was generally found only in books dealing with science fiction. But in 1957 an event took place that completely changed this. The Russians sent their first satellite, the Sputnick, into outer space. This both disturbed and excited the Americans who quickly took up the challenge.

During the next few years we saw many attempts made to explore the upper layers of our atmosphere. At first only instruments were sent into orbit. These were used to measure the physical conditions in deep outer space such as the amount of radiation. But very soon animals were being transported in satellites to determine what effects these physical conditions might have on man.

Then man was sent into space. People the world over listened and watched the progress of each astronaut from liftoff to splashdown. Before long teams of two and then three astronauts were being projected into space.

Finally, after a little over a decade from the launch of Sputnick, a team of three astronauts made a soft landing on the moon. What an exciting time this was for the world. Through the use of television cameras, people were able to actually see man's first step on the moon's surface.

Put the following on the posterboard strips.

| | | | |
|---|---|---|---|
| Sputnick is launched. | Sputnick is launched. | Man lands on the moon. | Instruments are the only cargo in the satellites. |
| Man lands on the moon. | Instruments are the only cargo in the satellites. | Animals are put into outer space. | Sputnick is launched. |
| Exploring space is still considered science fiction. | First man to orbit in a satellite. | First man to orbit in a satellite. | Man lands on the moon. |

## Student Game Directions:

1. Take the gameboard out of the box.

2. Read the story on the front of the gameboard.

3. Now unfold the board. *Do not* look back.

4. By moving the strips up and down, put the events in the correct order.

# Slippery Sequence

*(Intermediate)*

## Materials Needed:

posterboard—1 piece 6″ × 9″
            3 pieces 2½″ × 8″
ruler
scissors
felt-tipped pen

## Making the Game:

Cut 2½″ slits in the large piece of posterboard as shown below. Slide the posterboard strips in the slits.

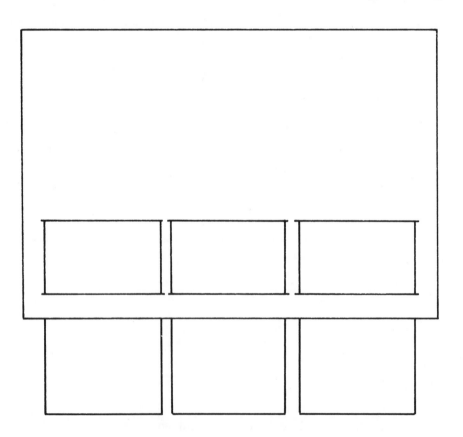

Put the following on the top of the large posterboard.

> A long time ago when our nation was still moving west, the settlers had to rely upon one another for survival. This was most apparent when a new family moved into the area. One of the first events to take place was a "barn raising."

Put the following on the posterboard strips. All three strips should be the same.

> While the men and the boys worked on the barn, the women and the girls busied themselves with the lunch preparations. Each family brought several dishes of specially prepared food so that lunchtime was truely a feast.
>
> Neighbors from miles around would come to help in the building. They would come early in the morning and bring the entire family. This was an event that everyone looked forward to.
>
> By evening everyone would gather on the new floor of the barn for some dancing. A fiddler would set the tempo and a square dance caller would organize the dancers into sets. The young children would stand around the sides, watching and clapping. Everyone had a grand time and the end of the day saw very tired but happy families heading for their homes.

## Student Game Directions:

1. Take the gameboard out of the box.

2. Read the paragraph on the large piece of posterboard.

3. There are three more paragraphs on each of the posterboard strips. It is up to you to slip the strips up and down, read the paragraphs, and put them in the correct order.

4. After you have done this, go back and read the whole story. Does it make sense?

5. Have someone check your answer.

# Newspaper Main Ideas

*(Intermediate)*

## Materials Needed:

newspaper stories
scissors

## Making the Game:

Cut out a variety of newspaper stories.

## Student Game Directions:

Locate and underline the main ideas in each paragraph.

# Following Directions

*(Intermediate)*

## Materials Needed:

posterboard—1 piece 8″ × 12″
                      piece 6″ × 6″
thin plain paper (newsprint)
felt-tipped pen

## Making the Game:

Put the following on the 8″ × 12″ piece of posterboard.

> 1. Place a piece of paper on the cardboard so that the cardboard is covered.
> 2. Make a large square, using the dots as a guide.
> 3. Draw two straight lines from the opposite corners of the square.
> 4. Darken in the upper triangle.
> 5. Put three dots in the triangle on the right side of the square.

Put the following on the 6″ × 6″ piece of posterboard.

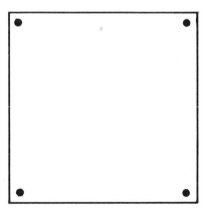

## Student Game Directions:

1. Read the direction card once or twice so that you know what you must do. Read it carefully.

2. Follow the directions. When you are finished have someone check your work.

# Newspaper Headings

*(Intermediate)*

## Materials Needed:

newspaper articles
scissors

## Making the Game:

Cut out a number of newspaper articles. Cut the heading off each article.

## Student Game Directions:

1. Separate the newspaper story from the titles.

2. Spread out the titles so that you can see all of them.

3. Read the story.

4. Look at the titles. Which one express the main idea of the story? Match the correct title with the story.

5. Have someone check your work.

# Why? Where? When?

*(Intermediate)*

## Materials Needed:

posterboard—8 pieces 2″ × 12″
                 8 pieces 2″ ×  3″
felt-tipped pen

## Making the Game:

Copy the following sentences on the 2″ × 12″ pieces of posterboard.

> The picture hung straight.
> In the evening they ate a snack.
> The dog romped playfully.
> He laid down in order to rest.
> The sun sank in the western sky.
> He was happy, so he laughed and laughed.
> The children swam in the river.
> It was early afternoon before the boys got out of bed.

Copy the following words on the 2″ × 3″ pieces of posterboard.

> HOW, WHEN, HOW, WHY, WHERE, WHY, WHERE, WHEN

## Student Game Directions:

1. Separate the sentence strips from the question word cards.

2. Read the sentence strips. Think of *how, where, when,* or *why* something occurred in each sentence.

3. If you can do number 2, then pick the correct question word card and match it with the sentence strip.

203

# Homograph Puzzle

*(Intermediate)*

## Materials Needed:

posterboard—12 pieces 4″ × 9″
  36 pieces 2″ × 3″
tape
felt-tipped pen

## Making the Game:

Set up a gameboard as follows:

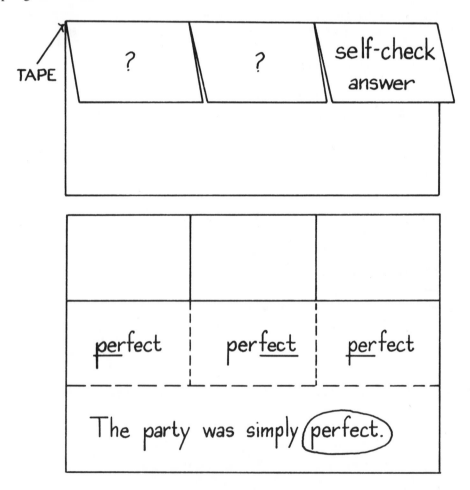

Tape three 2″ × 3″ posterboard pieces on each large piece as shown above.

204

Print the following sets of sentences and homographs on the 4″ × 9″ pieces of posterboard. Underscore the accented syllable as shown.

1. perfect   perfect   perfect
   The party was simply (perfect.)

2. protest   protest   protest
   The people wanted to (protest) the additional taxes.

3. convict   convict   convict
   He was a (convict) in a prison.

4. permit   permit   permit
   They received a fishing (permit) for Ohio.

5. compound   compound   compound
   The soldiers were restricted from leaving the (compound.)

6. subject   subject   subject
   Don't (subject) me to that boredom.

7. annex   annex   annex
   The department store kept the furniture in its (annex.)

8. rebel   rebel   rebel
   The teacher thought the boy was a (rebel.)

9. contract   contract   contract
   The girl had a (contract) to babysit over the summer.

10. combine   combine   combine
    The farmer used his (combine) to reap his harvest.

11. produce   produce   produce
    I found the lettuce in the (produce) department.

12. conduct   conduct   conduct
    The (conduct) of the class was excellent.

## Student Game Directions:

1. Take one of the gameboards out of the box.

2. Be sure that the flaps are down. Read the sentence. Pay particular attention to the circled word. This word may be pronounced two different ways. Decide which way is the correct way by raising the question mark flaps. Put stress on the part of the word that is underlined. After you have decided which is the correct word, lift the self-check flap to check your answer.

# Meaning Vocabulary

*(High Intermediate)*

## Materials Needed:

posterboard— 2 pieces 8″ × 12″

10 pieces 1″ × 3″

felt-tipped pen

## Making the Game:

Copy the following sentences on the large pieces of posterboard.

1. The boy was obviously a _____ at cooking.
2. She hung the _____ around her neck.
3. Bill was _____ to compete in the games.
4. The rains poured heavily and formed a _____ down the side of the mountain.
5. The _____ toured from village to village singing his songs.
6. The teacher asked him to _____ his story so that it would not be too long.
7. The general _____ his troops to form for attack.
8. The lion was so _____ that he frightened all the children at the zoo.
9. Jack's dog was very _____ .
10. The kidnappers held the boys for a high _____ .

Copy the following words on the small pieces of posterboard.

novice, medallion, reluctant, torrent, troubadour, abridge, bade, ferocious, obedient, ransom

## Student Game Directions:

1. Look at the sentences carefully. There is a word missing from each one.

2. Read the sentence leaving out the missing word.

3. Think of a word that might fit in the blank.

4. Pick a word from the word cards that you think will make sense.

5. Have someone check your work when you are done.

# 6 · Critical Reading Skills

While literal comprehension is necessary for the reader to understand what he or she has read, it is often necessary for the reader to go beyond this literal meaning. Writers often expect their readers to "read between the lines" or to "read beyond the lines." The author may write, "Bob clenched his fist," when he wants the reader to understand that Bob was angry. The author, in this case, expects his readers to read between the lines for the more sophisticated understanding.

Critical reading, as in comprehension, may be subdivided into various skill groups. The critical reading skills to be found in this section are:

Making Inferences
Developing Characterization
Making Judgments
Determining the Mood of the Story
Determining Fact from Opinion
Understanding Figurative Language

# Critical Reading Booklets

*(Primary–Intermediate)*

## Materials Needed:

old basal readers
scissors
stapler
construction paper
felt-tipped pen

## Making the Game:

Break the binding of the basals and tear out stories suitable for your students. Trim the edges and staple in a booklet fashion, using the construction paper as a cover.

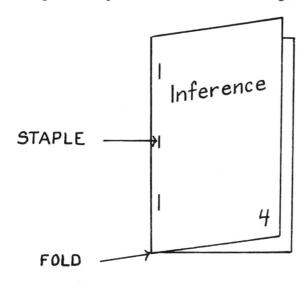

Put the skill on the cover and the ability level in the lower right corner.

On the inside of the back cover write out questions that will reinforce the skill you want to emphasize. The following are merely examples. You must formulate your own questions to correlate with the story.

*Inference*

Do you think Joe was upset with his friends? How could you tell?
Was the fight with the Indians necessary? What could have been done so that the fight could have been avoided?
Do you think Jim was dreaming? Why?

# Critical Reading Skills

*Characterization*

What characteristic of Chris is shown in the fact that he stomped off the football field?

Alice seemed to spend so much of her time looking into mirrors. What does this tell you about her personality?

How could you tell that Ferdinand was not like the other bulls?

*Making Judgments*

If it had not been so early in the morning what might the animals have done?

Was the story about a real or imaginary pony? How do we know?

Do you think that Alice dreamed this story or was it real?

*Mood of Story*

Did you feel happy or sad at the beginning of the story? Did this mood change by the end of the story?

How do you think Jim and Jerry felt at the birthday party?

*Fact from Opinion*

What did the teacher base his comments upon? Do you think his decision was fair?

*Figurative Language*

Locate an example of figurative language in the following pages.

What words did the author use to describe the fields of corn? What did he compare them to?

What simile helped you know the men were angry?

*Skimming*

Skim to find the portions of the story that tell the following:
1. How fierce the storm was.
2. Which boats returned to the harbor first.
3. What kind of fish the fishermen were catching.
Skim page 292 to find how many mountain climbers have scaled Mt. Everest.

## Student Game Directions:

1. Take one of the reading booklets out of the box.

2. Read it and answer the questions on the back cover.

# How Do You Feel?

*(Primary–Intermediate)*

## Materials Needed:

posterboard—4 pieces 9″ × 7″
                  4 pieces 3″ × 7″
scissors
ruler
glue or tape
felt-tipped pen

## Making the Game:

Cut the 3″ × 7″ pieces as shown. Fold the flaps using a ruler or straight edge so that they fold evenly.

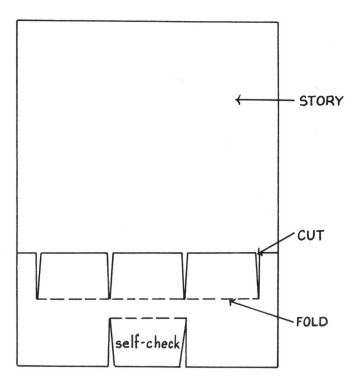

Glue or dry mount the 3″ × 7″ piece of posterboard on top of the large piece. It should be at the bottom as shown above. *Do not* glue the flaps!

Copy the following stories, one each, on the large posterboard pieces as shown above.

# Critical Reading Skills

Bend each flap up and copy the answers that are listed after each story. Don't forget to use the self-check.

*Story 1:*

The little house sat on the hill watching the white clouds leap-frogging across the sky. She could see the children in the distance climbing the old cherry tree. "My" she thought, "Summer is my favorite time of the year."

BRAVE   HAPPY   UPSET

*Story 2:*

The little house had not been taken care of for many years. Her paint was peeling and several of her windows were broken. No one had lived in her for such a long time that she could just barely remember the fun she used to have with the children.

GLAD   LAZY   SAD

*Story 3:*

It was a very dark night for the moon was hidden by the black clouds. "Oh," the little house thought, "I wish I wouldn't tremble so much on nights like this." But the wind whistling through the tree branches made such a moaning sound that she began to shake even more.

STRONG   FRIGHTENED   PLEASED

*Story 4:*

"Oh, dear," the little house wondered, "What are those men putting on my front lawn?" It looked like they were hammering in a sign. Then the little home knew it was a FOR SALE sign. This meant that her nice family would soon be moving out. She wondered what was to become of her.

UPSET   TIRED   SAFE

## Student Game Directions:

1. Take one of the gameboards out of the box.

2. Read the story. How do you think the house feels?

3. Lift flap A. Is this how you think the house feels? Lift flaps B and C.

4. When you think you have the right answer, lift the "self-check" flap and see if you are right.

# Fact or Fiction Wheels

*(High Primary–Low Intermediate)*

## Materials Needed:

posterboard—12 pieces 5″ × 7″
               24 pieces 1½″ × 1½″
scissors
felt-tipped pen

## Making the Game:

Cut car shapes from the 5″ × 7″ pieces of posterboard. Use the following form.

Cut circles from the small pieces of posterboard.

Copy the following sentences on the cars.

    The boys went fishing off the bridge.
    The girl was as small as your thumb.
    The old man lived in a cave.

The whale sang a very nice song.
The sun made the sidewalk very hot.
The moon winked at me.
The rooster strutted around the barnyard.
The house shook with fear.
The children danced because they were happy.
The horse flew high above the clouds.
The boys made a large fort out of the new fallen snow.
The giant drank the river dry.

On the back of each car write the word "Fact" or "Fiction" depending upon the sentence.

Print the word "Fact" on 12 of the wheels and the word "Fiction" on the other 12 wheels.

## Student Game Directions:

1. Take the cars out of the box.

2. Read one of the sentences. Could this really happen? If you think it could, place two "Fact" wheels on the car. If you think that it could never really happen, place two "Fiction" wheels on the car.

3. Continue to put wheels on all the cars.

4. In order to check your answers, turn the cars over.

# Sentence Ladder Game

*(High Primary–Intermediate)*

## Materials Needed:

posterboard—90 pieces 2″ by length of word, 15 pieces each in six different
colors of posterboard
felt-tipped pen

## Making the Game:

Print the following words on the posterboard.

| GREEN | ORANGE | WHITE | BLUE | RED | YELLOW |
|-------|--------|-------|------|-----|--------|
| a | by | one | hop | hug | alone |
| a | do | two | fell | huge | sick |
| an | could | three | jump | boy | crowd |
| it | cause | four | running | ski | well |
| it | since | five | ride | mountain | mailman |
| if | with | six | road | farm | pilot |
| if | not | seven | jumped | ripple | conductor |
| this | didn't | eight | jumping | village | dancer |
| the | did | nine | fling | little | actor |
| the | have | ten | flew | valley | actress |
| there | couldn't | eleven | danced | ocean | people |
| that | because | twelve | walk | sea | building |
| their | don't | thirteen | walking | forest | lady |
| what | so | fourteen | walked | scuba | man |
| and | should | fifteen | ran | jungle | elevator |

## Student Game Directions:

1. Two people play this game at a time.

2. Choose someone to go first.

3. Make a sentence using no more than twelve words. You can use only those words on
   the posterboard pieces. The different colors are worth different points.

215

green = 1 point
orange = 2 points
white = 3 points
blue = 4 points
red = 5 points
yellow = 6 points

4. When you have finished a sentence, count up the total number of points your sentence is worth.

5. Now the other person tries to make a sentence worth more points.
   You can try as many times as you like!

# Make a Monster of a Sentence

*(High Primary–Intermediate)*

## Materials Needed:

posterboard—5 pieces 7″ × 11″; each piece must be a different color
scissors
felt-tipped pen

## Making the Game:

Cut the following designs from *each* of the five pieces of posterboard.

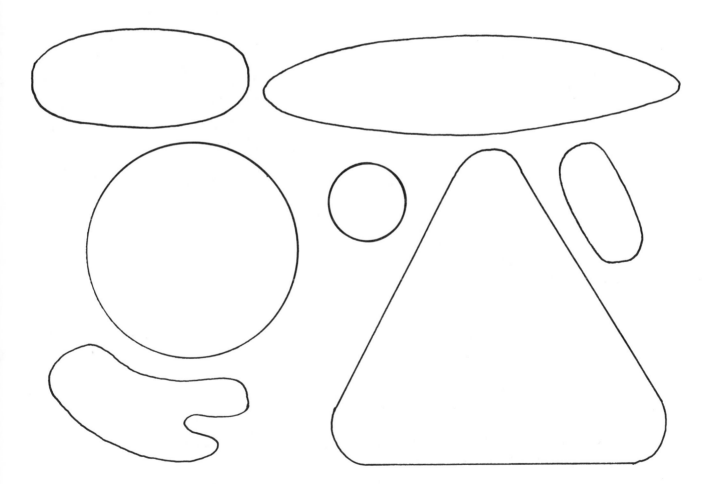

217

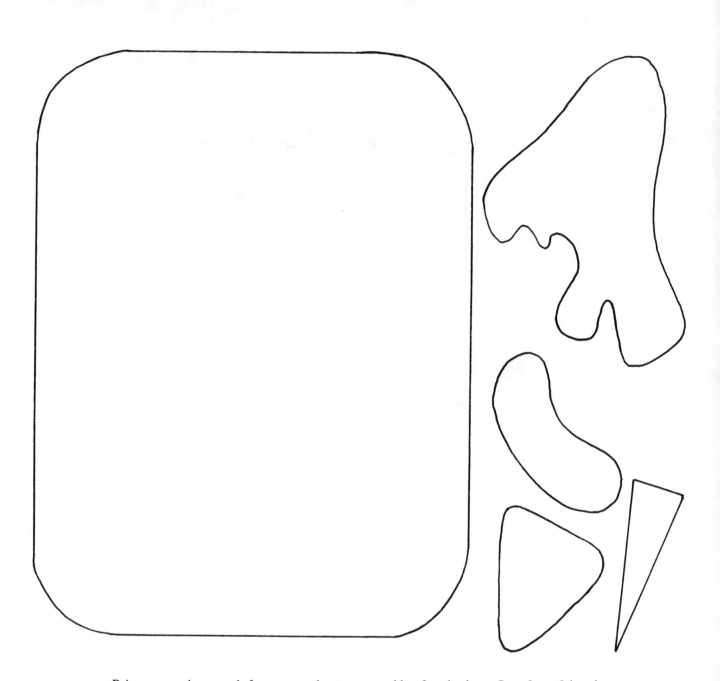

Print appropriate words for your students on one side of each piece. On a few of the pieces put a large X.

## Student Game Directions:

1. Place all the pieces on your desk with the blank side showing.

2. Your job is to make some "wild" monster using the shapes.

3. When you have finished, turn the pieces over. Now you must "make a monster of a sentence" using every word that is on your monster pieces. You may use more words than are on the pieces, but you *must* use all the words on your pieces. Some pieces have X's. If you're lucky enough to have chosen an X, you simply decide upon the word you want to use in your sentence.

# Appendix

## HOMONYMS

write-right-rite
stationery-stationary
marry-merry
flue-flu-flew
plane-plain
pail-pale
wait-weight
choo-chew
principal-principle
pair-pare-pear
cite-sight-site
choose-chews
capital-capitol
lean-lien
past-passed
sent-cent-scent
guest-guessed
need-knead
wave-waive
close-clothes
buy-by
know-no
be-bee
blue-blew
maid-made
their-there-they're
meet-meat
peer-pier
higher-hire
shone-shown
tea-tee
teem-team
beat-beet
sore-soar
grown-groan
but-butt
prey-pray
ring-wring
hail-hale
horse-hoarse

hear-here
rode-road
fairy-ferry
real-reel
ant-aunt
main-mane-Maine
die-dye
bore-boar
course-coarse
fair-fare
pause-paws
piece-peace
pour-poor
lye-lie
mist-missed
mail-male
thrown-throne
sleight-slate
knight-night
dough-doe
red-read
would-wood
we-wee
ate-eight
sail-sale
air-heir
feet-feat
sun-son
way-weigh
do-dew-due
peel-peal
eye-I-aye
shear-sheer
soul-sole
vale-veil
stare-stair
loan-lone
dear-deer
nun-none
load-lode

threw-through
new-knew-gnu
great-grate
bear-bare
week-weak
not-knot
you-ewe
tear-tier
hair-hare
tow-toe
clause-claws
seem-seam
rain-reign-rein
sense-cents-scents
bough-bow
creek-creak
very-vary
waist-waste
seen-scene
heal-heel
nose-knows
to-two-too
see-sea
for-four-fore
pain-pane
bred-bread
shoe-shoo
one-won
steel-steal
flee-flea
heard-herd
stake-steak
lain-lane
mite-might
tale-tail
so-sew
sewn-sown
tic-tick
hour-our
hole-whole

# *Appendix*

## ANTONYMS

| | | |
|---|---|---|
| sweet-sour | dirty-clean | take-give |
| prince-princess | sick-well | happy-sad |
| black-white | hard-soft | round-square |
| dangerous-safe | honesty-deceit | dark-light |
| morning-evening | summer-winter | short-tall |
| everything-nothing | ill-healthy | fat-thin |
| children-adults | borrow-loan | late-early |
| sunrise-sunset | brother-sister | quiet-noisy |
| same-different | together-apart | for-against |
| strange-familiar | son-daughter | always-never |
| bold-cowardly | male-female | fingers-toes |
| deep-shallow | shout-whisper | gigantic-wee |
| simple-complex | straight-crooked | before-after |
| brave-scared | engine-caboose | plain-fancy |
| niece-nephew | pointed-rounded | north-south |
| proud-humble | narrow-wide | stretch-shrink |
| rough-smooth | empty-full | awake-asleep |
| pretty-ugly | alive-dead | sharp-dull |
| smile-frown | stay-leave | young-old |
| day-night | good-bad | true-false |
| here-there | all-none | throw-catch |
| work-play | king-queen | husband-wife |
| big-little | best-worst | small-large |
| sunny-rainy | arm-leg | will-won't |
| head-foot | old-new | tell-listen |
| under-over | girl-boy | you-me |
| aunt-uncle | high-low | in-out |
| raw-cooked | push-pull | near-far |
| lead-follow | sun-moon | salt-pepper |
| dim-bright | need-have | real-fake |
| enter-exit | won-lost | yes-no |
| top-bottom | hot-cold | rich-poor |
| close-open | fast-slow | run-walk |
| back-front | few-many | stop-go |
| lost-found | buy-sell | wet-dry |
| weak-strong | easy-hard | woman-man |
| left-right | came-went | east-west |
| long-short | begin-end | up-down |
| cool-warm | stand-sit | first-last |
| laugh-cry | black- white | off-on |

## COMPOUND WORDS

| | | |
|---|---|---|
| snowshoe | policeman | fishhook |
| snowman | footman | seashore |
| snowflake | watchman | seaport |
| snowfight | fisherman | seashell |
| snowstorm | milkman | seaplane |
| snowplow | doorman | oceanfront |
| dollhouse | chairman | oceanliner |
| doghouse | typewriter | bedtime |
| greenhouse | whichever | nighttime |
| playhouse | whenever | daytime |
| courthouse | notebook | anytime |
| birdhouse | schoolbook | rainbow |
| farmhouse | pocketbook | clockwise |
| lighthouse | workbook | counterclockwise |
| henhouse | cookbook | baseball |
| schoolhouse | textbook | basketball |
| schoolyard | bookmark | football |
| playground | bookworm | neighborhood |
| playpen | bookcase | handwriting |
| today | bookkeeper | supermarket |
| tonight | bookstore | handbag |
| into | storybook | filmstrip |
| something | everything | cowboy |
| sometimes | everyone | cowgirl |
| somewhere | drugstore | pigsty |
| somehow | paperback | sandbox |
| someone | horseback | hatbox |
| anybody | bareback | playmate |
| anything | nowhere | teammate |
| anyway | cupcake | classmate |
| anyhow | shortbread | classroom |
| anyplace | gingerbread | cannot |
| anywhere | grandfather | tiptoe |
| bedside | grandmother | lunchroom |
| butterfly | sidewalk | bedroom |
| battlefield | inside | bathroom |
| firearms | outside | stoplight |
| fireside | beside | meanwhile |
| sailboat | mountainside | barnyard |
| lifeboat | cornfield | proofread |
| mailman | armchair | firewood |
| fireman | fireplace | silkworm |
| spaceman | blacksmith | championship |
| sandman | broomstick | worldwide |
| bellhop | rainstorm | bathtub |
| motorboat | nightmare | redcap |

221

afternoon
handmade
handsome
airport
airplane
airline
headband
headmaster
bluebird
blackbird
hummingbird
uptown
downtown
downstairs
crosswalk
however
catfish
swordfish
jellyfish
starfish
kingfish
shoreline
coastline
steamshovel
steamboat
steamroller
doughnut
automobile
newspaper
newsprint
armchair
hallway
jackknife
fullback
broadcast
birthstone
hairbrush
bluebell
waterproof
brainstorm
bridegroom
daredevil
buttermilk
highway
candlestick
keyhole

network
dishcloth
dishwater
dishpan
dishtowel
pancake
shortstop
pitchfork
shoehorn
shipwreck
footstep
underground
railroad
snapdragon
bullfrog
headlight
grapefruit
pineapple
graveyard
hitchhike
milkweed
sandpaper
sunflower
toothpaste
toothbrush
toothache
shoestring
shoelace
shoemaker
oilcloth
landlord
windmill
porthole
otherwise
popcorn
Thanksgiving
dugout
birthday
blastoff
goldenrod
loophole
footstool
dragonfly
bulldog
butterscotch
yardstick

doorbell
backdoor
blackberry
strawberry
blueberry
gooseberry
grapevine
countdown
sunshine
bedroll
bedspread
battleship
friendship
oatmeal
scorekeeper
workshop
highway
eyebrow
eyelid
eyesight
haystack
cardboard
overboard
lonesome
driveway
streamline
nightgown
grasshopper
moonlight
understood
streetcar
tablecloth
blueprint
necktie
maybe
manpower
housewife
birthplace
fingernails
bodyguard
numberline
breakdown
grandstand
bandstand
buttercup
campsite
dressmaker

_Appendix_

## CONTRACTIONS

| | | |
|---|---|---|
| I'll | they'd | let's |
| he'll | you'd | who's |
| she'll | I've | who'd |
| it'll | we've | who'll |
| we'll | you've | what's |
| they'll | aren't | what'd |
| you'll | isn't | what'll |
| I'm | haven't | where's |
| he's | hasn't | where'd |
| she's | didn't | where'll |
| it's | doesn't | that's |
| we're | don't | that'd |
| they're | wasn't | that'll |
| you're | weren't | there's |
| I'd | wouldn't | there'd |
| he'd | won't | there'll |
| she'd | couldn't | how's |
| it'd | can't | how'd |
| we'd | shouldn't | how'll |